MW01168969

Never Give Up
The Autobiography of a Survivor of Ritual Abuse and Mind Control

Part One

Copyright 2024

Dedicated to the brave survivors around the world who have worked to get free of cult and mind control abuse, and the wonderful people who support them. Thank you.

Also, to the One who has made my journey out of the cult possible and given me the courage to share the things written within these pages: the true Jesus Christ.

Foreword

For the last thirty years, I served in the field of trauma recovery, first as a clinical therapist and later, as a prayer minister with a specialty in helping survivors recover from ritual abuse. I believe the field owes svali a huge debt of gratitude for her latest contribution of *Never Give Up.* I so appreciate the brave and difficult sharing of her life story and the sheer courage it has taken her to stand up against such evil in order to shed light on how the sophisticated techniques of mind control shape and indoctrinate a child into loyal devotion to her cult group. Svali takes us through her childhood journey that is actually no childhood but is more like one nightmare after another until she begins to question what she is being told and forced to do that is so incongruent with her heart. We, both survivor and helper, benefit from her labor of love in sharing her story with us. Survivors can receive insight into their own stories from one of the best explained examples of cult indoctrination I have read. Survivors can witness how mind control is accomplished as well as use the examples in this book for validation of their own similar memories and experiences. Helpers receive valuable information about the complexities of cult abuse, what struggles a survivor will likely encounter to risk breaking free and the astounding service gaps in our culture to aid survivors to break free.

This book is not an "easy read". While the stories are shared with captivating details that will keep the reader's interest, the stories of human tragedy and disregard for human life makes this difficult to absorb and the reader is left with wonderment at what causes such evil in our society. As a Christian prayer minister, I believe that our battle is not against flesh and blood but against spiritual forces of darkness. Satan's tactics are exposed by svali in the stories she recalls. Svali describes the methods used by the trainers to accomplish their purposes which are inspired by the dark forces the cult group calls the "Immortals", the spirits they serve and worship. At one point, svali points out that Satan and his minions cannot force humans to do anything against their will but must have agreement from humans to accomplish his evil plans. In numerous examples, svali shares how her trainers work with her agreement to coax her into accepting what she is participating in. From these stories, we receive insights into generational patterns in cults of agreeing to perform dark deeds out of fear of reprisal from the trainers, out of a belief of needing to obey to survive and/or protect other's lives from destruction, and a deceptive redefinition of immortality perpetuating a belief of superiority that there are those worthy to live and those who are expendable.

Satan must deceive, seduce and terrify humans into cooperating with him. He must also work within the needs and desires of the human race to entice compliance from his subjects. The trainers simply use rewards and punishments to reinforce a child's need to survive and to be loved, accepted, belong and feel special to someone. Svali's descriptions of how these basic attachment needs are manipulated and used by the cult trainers provide sharp clarity for understanding how a child is controlled into cooperating through working hard to numb and dissociate while preforming abhorrent tasks of torture on other human beings in order to achieve the trainer's praise, attention and affection and avoid their severely punishing responses for disobedience. If the trainers only used fear and intimidation to force obedience from their subjects, the fear would not be sustained and the training would fail. These sophisticated trainers know that the manipulation of attachment needs is crucial to establish loyalty in their subjects. As the Bible says, "love never fails" and a child will do whatever it takes for love even for occasional moments of love doled out to them according to the trainer's strict schedule.

There is no greater human motivator than love. Love is what drove svali for years to serve a group with which she increasingly became disillusioned. But through it all there was another One who was pursuing her with love and He never let her go. This is a story ultimately about unfailing love. In this first book that describes parts of her early childhood, svali slaves for the scraps of love that are given to her under conditional terms from her trainers. Even so that love is powerful enough to harness her attachment and loyalty until a greater unconditional love begins to break through to her and call her out of the entrapment of the cult environment. In the second book of her story, *Never Give Up*, of her teen years and adulthood, svali will share much more on how the unconditional love of God pursues her, forgives and restores her, and keeps pursuing her until she finds the strength to break free.

In her pursuit of freedom, svali found very little help from the outside world to break free. Of all the various groups of people in the world, I can think of few others more in need of resources and help than those escaping mind control cults and yet there are so few good resources. Part of the difficulty has been a lack of education and understanding of how difficult it is to break away and how much opposition the survivor typically endures from their groups. After reading svali's story, we readers can no longer claim a limited understanding for our lack of response. I heard svali say once that she believed there would be a mass exodus from the cult if survivors of cults knew there was a place for them to belong outside their groups with people who would love and care about them. I hope that svali's labor of love to us through sharing her difficult story will be the impetus to cause others to open their hearts and doors to survivors in their homes, churches, and communities to begin to provide the greatly needed resources for their freedom.

"Evil persists when good men do nothing." Edmund Burke

Jo Getzinger, MSW
C.A.R.E., Inc.
www.care1@triton.net

Contents

Introduction 11

    Defining Some Terms Used in this Book 16

Chapter 1: Infancy 25

    Josef Mengele's Cruelty 28

    Survival of the Fittest 30

    Sexual Training 35

    Bonding to the Fathers 40

    The Drawer 45

    Learning to Crawl Towards Colored Lights 47

    Early Training and Assessment 52

    Angel in the Labs 55

    Learning to Stay on the Path 57

    Failure to Thrive 63

Chapter 2: Early Spiritual Training 68

    Meeting the Immortals 68

    Celestial Heaven 70

    Mortal Hell 76

    The Destruction of the Universe 85

    The Council of the Flesh and the Council of the Immortals
    89

Chapter 3: Toddlerhood 94

Control the Children 96

The Cages..102

Alice in Wonderland...107

Shell Programming...122

Chapter 4: Theta and Spiritual Systems Training 130

Theta Training 130

Spiritual Systems Training.................................136

Q'bala Training...136

Egyptian 139

Babylonian 143

Druidic...144

Ancients 150

Theo...159

Satan's Throne 162

Chapter 5: Other Memories................................169

Being programmed to be a 'presenter' 169

Learning to do sacrifices 175

Learning to Play Chess 179

The German Father's House 181

A German Christmas 186

Chapter 6: Military and Academic Training.......................191

Starting School...191

Anatomy Class...193

History and Political Classes............................197

Baby Soldiers (Military Training) 201

Climbing the Mountain and Teamwork 205

Break Time and Pranks 212

Chapter 7: Learning to Become a Mage...............216

The Elements 221

Traveling Dimensions.....................................223

Power battles..226

Shape Shifting 228

Chapter 8: Learning to Become an Agent 235

First Mission...235

MI6...239

Learning to Take on a Pack of Dogs 242

Sex Parties..246

Early Testing...252

Chapter 9: A Walk in the Garden 258

Remember the Flowers...................................266

Chapter 10: Learning to Become a Trainer 271

Chapter 11: Christmas in the Vatican..................288

Chapter 12: The Gift of the Magi 294

Chapter 13: Coming of Age 298

Chapter 14: Wedded to Satan..............................306

Afterword 311

About the Author..313

Introduction

I remember being told, when I was a very young child, to say the words, with other children, "Ich bin eine kinder macht zachens gut" (I am a child who does things well). I believed it then, because life really was about performing well. But now, as I am older, I realize that this was not really true. I was a child who desperately wanted to be loved.

This is an autobiography in which I describe parts of the first twelve years of my life growing up in a highly organized and extremely wealthy occultic group: the Jesuit Order. Their wealth enables them to build extremely sophisticated programming studios and laboratories, and to use and develop advanced healing and mind control technologies. This autobiography does not include all memories, of course, since that would require a library of books. Instead, I share the memories that stand out the most from these early years. It is thus a "snapshot" of various scenes I lived through as a child to show what it was like to experience these events. While in previous books, I have discussed programming more from the observer perspective, in this book, I am much more personal.

This book is not written in chronological order. The first chapter covers a few key milestones in my infancy. The remaining chapters are grouped according to topic, and cover memories from various ages within that topic. In these chapters, I often share how early trauma and training lay the foundations for later programming and training for the skill area or job discussed in that chapter.

I realize that some of the memories I share, especially in the mage and spiritual training sections, may be hard to believe. I may be accused of having read too many 'fantasy novels' (which I never have and never will read since they have always frightened me). I believe that instead, some (but, of course, not all) writers in that genre may be actually drawing from their memories of these types of things. I am also aware that some of the events I describe can be attributed to cult members dressed in costumes in elaborate setups, the use of virtual reality, drugs and hypnosis and other forms of trickery.

However, I also believe that not all things that occur in our world can be explained this simply. I believe that there is a spiritual, or even unknowable element to some experiences, i.e., encounters with forces that defy material or rational explanation. All that I can do is to share for the record my own encounters with these beings according to how I experienced these events, alongside the memories of the more mundane and very physical events of my childhood growing up in an occult training facility.

My memories are not unique. Many survivors around the world from various cults and agencies that practice mind control have reported similar things, including the military and assassin training, the training to respond to visual codes, tones, colors and other cues; spiritual training, and being wedded to Satan. None of these training and events are unique to the Jesuit order, although methods may vary from those used in other groups.

I have heard concerns that sharing memories about programming is giving too much information, possibly providing a "blueprint" for "how to program people." I do not agree because programming involves much more than reading how one group does things. Reading memories of how one organized group programs their members, and then being able to program others, i.e., elicit the desired behaviors and beliefs in the subject, would be similar to reading a book on quantum physics, and then being able to build a spaceship. It simply can't be done. A lot more knowledge and skill are required to be able to program people than is described in this book. Additionally, the groups capable of conducting the kind of programming described in this book are already doing the things described here, since this is from fifty years ago and things have advanced exponentially since then.

I have written this autobiography for several reasons. One is to expose what is going on in a world that is increasingly confronting what can simply be termed as "evil", and some of the experiences that produce people capable of this evil. I also want to validate the memories of those who have survived similar types of abuse. I describe the impacts of such abuse on a young child and over that person's lifetime, and hope that this would be helpful not only to survivors, but also to therapists and others who support survivors. To emphasize hope and the incredible strength and capacity for humanity that survivors retain despite pervasive early abuse, I share too how I began to question and break free of the abuse and control, despite my years of indoctrination, trauma and mind-controlled, programmed obedience to the Order where I had perpetrated against others under orders.

In the book I describe several memories of the Order investing tremendous amounts of time, effort, manpower and finances on the spiritual training and spiritually-themed programming of their infants and children. Some readers may ask, "Why on earth do they go to such a great lengths to instill occult beliefs in their children?" The answer is that the Jesuit Order in its dark side completely believes in the concepts of ascension (into immortality, bliss and fulfilment) and descension (into mortality and hell). Religion is a great motivator, as seen historically and around the world, and the Jesuits are no exception. They are fervent in their beliefs in ascension and descension to a degree that would put to shame many of the most fervent believers in many faiths. They spend a great deal of time passing their beliefs on to each new generation, as my memories illustrates, and believe that children must be introduced very early to these concepts in order to fully believe and grasp such concepts. As very young children learn best through concrete experiences, they train and program children through the use of older cult members dressed up as spiritual entities, and take them through studios designed to look like locations in the spiritual realms or dimensions. They believe that without these early concrete experiences, the child when older will eventually have much greater difficulty in accessing the dimensions, and seeing, hearing and interacting with immortal beings who assist with ascension.

Finally, this is my personal story. As human beings, we each long for someone to hear our story, whether good or bad, as this is part of the processing that occurs for those who have survived extreme trauma. In a sense, this is my narrative shared with the world now, in hopes that it will accomplish some good, and provide some hope for others who long to be free.

The memories shared within these pages are the result of 35 years of working at healing. These memories did not come forward quickly, easily or painlessly. It involved many years of journaling, therapy, prayer ministry, using dolls and other toys to act out what had happened, as well as other modalities. Over time, I have gained a much better understanding of what my life was, and as a result, what I want to rest of my life to be. I want it to be free of the manipulation, the demands for performance, and the spiritual darkness that characterized my younger years. My greatest desire is to now live my life in thanksgiving to the God of the Bible, and His son, Jesus, who have forgiven me for the terrible – and painful – things I was forced to do, throughout my life.

Defining Some Terms Used in this Book

Dissociation and Programming: When a person is subjected to extreme pain to the degree that his/her mental, emotional or physical survival is threatened, that person can **dissociate**, i.e., create a new state of consciousness that is capable of doing anything in order to survive or stop the trauma. Emotional traumas, such as abandonment, even in the absence of physical traumas, especially by an attachment figure, can also cause dissociation. This new state of consciousness is extremely suggestible. Programmers in the cults consider this a type of *tabula rasa* state: in order to survive, this new state of consciousness will believe/do/feel whatever it is told to think/do/feel and is easily convinced that this compliance is what stops the abusers from abusing him/her. Common terms for these new states of consciousness include "personalities", "parts" or "alters". The goal of cult-controlled dissociation as described in these pages is to **'program'** the child: (1) subject a young child to enough pain, physical or mental, or both, to create new states, (2) give them names or codes, (3) teach these new states specific beliefs, emotions and/or jobs, (4) condition these parts into continued compliance by reward and punishment. In this book, I use the term **'parts'**.

Cult host: the cult host is the part of the child raised in a cult who lives the child's cult life, e.g., this is the part who is out in the body during rituals, meetings and lessons in the cult facilities, and so on. This part will not be amnesic to the cult activities. For me, this was the part of me that felt most substantial and most like the "real me" since most of my life was spent in cult facilities or carrying out duties for the cult in other settings.

Presenter: In the Jesuit order, these are the parts of an individual that are created to be "out", or to present and live in the "normal world" in "ordinary families" outside the training facility. These parts are programmed to present in various countries, and will have families that host them starting at age three. Each presenter in each country will have been programmed to have its own name, personality, abilities and preferences, and to be completely amnesic to all cult activities, as well as to the activities of the other presenter parts. Despite being one set of parts, they will believe that they are the entire person, and only recall an ordinary life with no hint of any cult existence. Presenter parts are typically programmed to disbelieve, deny, or be highly distressed by any cult-related memories.

Internalize: During early childhood, we tend to internalize the things we experience and see (building a sense of reality and how the world works). Programmers take advantage of this natural developmental period to introduce parts to concrete experiences that demonstrate to the child the scenarios, people and beliefs that they want the child to internalize. For instance, if they want the child to internalize a castle, they will take the child to spend time in this castle. If they want the child to develop an internal 'castle guard', they will have a designated part spend time with a castle guard (to role model the beliefs and behaviors), then dress the part up as a castle guard and have the part act out this role. This kind of 'internalization' is common across individuals who experience early trauma, for instance, the person who realizes that they still hear their critical parents' voices inside their heads long after they have attained adulthood. Due to the dissociation, parts subject to these setups may only have experiences of the 'reality' that their programmers had them 'experience'.

Programming studio: These are large dedicated rooms or areas for programming in the cult facilities. These studios would rival the best of any Hollywood filming studio. They can be designed to look like any place that the programmers need, e.g., space ships, pyramids, underwater caverns, the city of Troy, a circus, etc. They have state-of-the-art lighting, animatronics, holograms, walls, ceiling, and floors that are screens that can display any scenario, and other audio-visual technologies to create extremely realistic experiences for the child being programmed in them. During programming scenarios, the adults and older children will put on costumes and act out the scenes (for instance, in a 'hell' scene, they may dress up as demons) that the programmers want the infants and children to learn about and eventually internalize.

Programming laboratories: Often located in the same buildings as the programming studios, these are areas dedicated to research on programming, and where children and adults receive assessments, health checkups, programming schedules and other processes that are critical to their programming. Very sophisticated equipment for programming, data collection, data management and so on is part of these labs.

The Fathers: Individuals in the Jesuit Order, both men and women, (yes, there are both sexes in the occultic side of this order, unlike the male only fathers in the public side) who have undergone the full training required and completed the coming of age ceremony at age 13 (described later in this book), are titled 'fathers'. For instance, as a child, I called my primary mentor, "Father Mattheo".

The Fathers I Loved: As the Order understands the importance of attachment and community for mind control, each child raised in the Order will be given 12 primary Fathers to be bonded to from infancy. Three of these 12 will be designed as the child's primary programmers, and the child will be conditioned to bond most strongly with these three fathers. This bonding starts in the womb, then throughout infancy and childhood. It is common for individuals in the Order to be assigned three new primary programmers as they become adults. This is to ensure that the person continues to be bonded to agents capable of controlling them as their original programmers age, and that there is no risk of losing control over that individual should their original programmers die. These new programmers are typically selected from among peers who he/she is already very close to, such as a twin, a classmate (who is as close to them as any biological sister or brother could be), or a close mentor.

Class: At the age of six, children raised in the Jesuit programming facilities are assigned to a class consisting of eleven other children their own age, to create a group of twelve for each class. There are multiple classes within each facility, and each class will have their own dormitory. These children eat together, sleep together, go to classes together, go through physical training together, and bond extremely closely to one another. The fathers tell them that they are "sisters" and "brothers". The children consider their classmates to be sisters and brothers, emotionally, even if not genetically. Along with the fathers, these classmates comprise the child's "family" when growing up in the facility.

Mage: The Jesuit Order is very occultic. Each child will have spiritual mentors who have achieved the status of a mage, an individual who has become extremely well versed in occultic knowledge, incantations, spells, and rituals over many years of training, intense study and testing. Mages are expected to mentor those younger than them, and to help raise up a new generation of mages. They are skilled in oral teaching, ancient languages and are often master storytellers, since much of the information is also passed down in oral form. All children are expected to become mages themselves. I use the term 'mage' instead of other terms for practitioners of the occult arts, such as 'wizard', 'sorcerer', 'magician' or 'witch' as this is the term that parts used when sharing their memories.

Ascended Master: This is considered by the Jesuits the highest form of spiritual achievement. These individuals are considered as close to ascension as a human being can achieve while still walking the earth.

Immortal: The Order believe that immortals are beings who are trying to help mankind ascend and become like them, and to teach them how to overcome their mortal flesh. "Overcoming the mortal flesh" includes suppressing the desires within a human being that make them flinch away from interacting with these beings, and accepting the pain and long, difficult training that the fathers believe is necessary to ascend. The Jesuit fathers utterly and completely believe in these immortals, and in the theology of ascension and descension.

Demon: I believe that the immortals and other spiritual beings described in this book are actually demons, or what the Bible describes as fallen angels. These beings were formerly filled with glory and were in the presence of the true God of the Bible. However, the one named Lucifer (now known as "Satan") chose to rebel against the loving creator of the universe, due to pride (he wanted to be as God). In his rebellion, the Bible says that one third of the angels followed Lucifer and became fallen angels, or demons are they are commonly known. Demons can also refer in some theologies to the souls of individuals or Nephilim who are wandering the earth. In my book, I am not referring to this interpretation, but instead, to the "fallen angel" definition. While I believe that both angels and demons are real, as the memories in this book make clear, some of the "demons" I encountered in childhood were actually older children or adults in costumes. Also, I had many parts who were programed to believe they were demons. This is extremely common in ritual abuse and mind control groups. These parts are usually very young children. These parts, when they came out, would growl, threaten, and act very convincingly according to how people believe demons would act. In reality, however, they were frightened little children who had been given a difficult role to play inside, whether as a punisher, a guardian, or other jobs.

Chapter 1: Infancy

One of my first memories is of looking at the light sifting in through an outside window. I am an infant, and am being held, and allowed to look outside for a brief moment. I am old enough to hold my head up and body straight, as I peer longingly at the outside world, at the soft greens, browns and blues of grass, earth and sky. I wonder if even then, I was longing to be free from the facility that was almost my whole world the first three years of life.

I was conceived in a genetics laboratory in Switzerland, the product of "state of the art" genetic manipulation. I was a "generation 3" baby in the Order, from one of the batches of genetically designed babies that were 'benefiting' from their latest round – the third one - of genetic knowledge, including the ability to isolate genes for intelligence, strength, and quick healing. I know this from looking later in life at my own records, once I had clearance at the cult facility as a trainer myself. As an adult in the Order, I also read my own records of the programming done to me while in utero, but I have no conscious memories of the programming; only vague, inchoate feelings of rage, sadness, joy, love and rejection, and feeling very disturbed at the thought of what these feelings could mean.

All I can really be sure of is that as a fetus, my life was unpleasant and manipulated, a mixture of reward and punishment, to prepare me for what was to come when I was born. What was distressingly omitted was something I had never known, but instinctively craved: real love without conditions. It was to become a deep longing throughout my life. Later in life, after I left the Order, during my healing journey I met fetal parts from the prenatal period of my life. These fetal parts had not only their original memories, but had also been programmed throughout my lifespan. This made their memories a mix of primal fetal rage, fear, and pain due to early traumas, and the meaning their programmers gave these memories.

My next conscious memory, a brief flash, is of being held lovingly by a woman who is rocking me in a chair, while she nurses me at her breast. The room is white; the woman is dressed in white, and she is singing me a song about how the best and bravest do great things for the Order, smiling tenderly at me the whole time. I am content, and love her, this woman who is one of my primary trainers, as she soothes me after a programming session that I no longer remember, or want to remember, wanting simply to experience being held and loved for this point in time. There is no other type of love available, so like a sponge, I soak it up.

Another memory flash: men in white lab coats come through the nursery, checking each infant. I am in a metal crib with bars, and want to get out, but I am still too young to try. But even then, the thought of escape, while unattainable then, simmers in the back of my mind. The problem is that it is getting fuzzier, a bit harder each day, to know exactly what it is that I want to escape, but even during rest, I feel deep within that something is very wrong here, something that I need to get away from, regardless of the soothing words and loving pats on the back.

I want to note here that early trainers are both male and female, and in the facility that I was raised in, female trainers often nursed young infants as part of the bonding, and also to comfort them after stressful training sessions. The trainers were sometimes given injections of hormones to lactate if they were not actively lactating. The Jesuit fathers were well aware of the importance of attachment in development, and in programming. The fathers who programmed me were dissociative as well; there was a tradition of abuse that created dissociation for many centuries in the Order. The love and nurturing they showed was real; it was not "fake", but it was still manipulative, because they were not free to love the way that I believe many of them longed to. They were all slaves to fear – the fear of disobeying Satan – and this fear made them unable to love in a truly free or healthy manner. What they did instead was to pour out the love within them in the carefully prescribed ways that were permitted, such as when holding and nursing the babies. When I was older, this was one of the ways I was allowed to be tender, and I loved cuddling and holding the babies. Even in this terribly abusive environment, the members of our group found ways to express love whenever we could.

Josef Mengele's Cruelty

I am in the infant nursery at some point later in time. There are dozens of us infants in this room. We are in little metal cribs with metal rails, on mattresses with white sheets. We all wear little white soft long shirts and linen diapers, and can see each other through the bars of our cribs, or when we pull ourselves up to stand and peek over. Today, one of the other babies in the nursery is pulling himself up, and is energetically trying to climb over the raised rail of his crib. Interested, I pull myself upright, using the rail of my crib, to get a better view of what he is doing. He tries to climb over, drops back, then keeps trying, until finally, he falls right over onto the white tiled floor with a "thump!"

All of us other babies stare, and wonder if we can do the same; it looks like fun! The baby who escaped happily crawls around to the other cribs, as if urging us to join him. He seems to act a bit triumphant and proud of himself. Then, he crawls towards the main door to the nursery, which seems to be the way out since that is where all the trainers go through when they leave. Suddenly, footsteps are heard, the door swings open, and an enraged Mengele comes stomping into the nursery. His glasses and hair are quivering with rage.

He yanks the little boy baby on the floor up by one arm, and takes him over to a large wooden table in the middle of the room. He takes a large steel cleaver off a nearby table, and suddenly he chops the infant's hands off on the table top, with loud "thunks". All of us other infants stare at this scene with wide eyes of horror. We are silent, too terrified to even scream. Then, Mengele takes the little boy baby, and hangs him upside down from a hook in the middle of the nursery, to bleed to death in front of us all. The blood drips down, and the terrified baby screams as his white shirt turns scarlet, until finally, his cries slowly stop as the life ebbs out of him in spurts.

During this act of dying, Mengele glares at the rest of us infants, and screams in German, "This is what happens to "bad babies" who don't obey or try to get away!" Terrified at what I have just witnessed, shaking inside, I decide then not to try to crawl out of my crib, regardless of how wrong things feel in this place. I decide to bury these feelings of wanting to escape deep inside, because I very much want to live. Being the object of Mengele's anger is a very, very bad situation to be in, and I try to conform to what he wants as best as I can, even at this young age.

Mengele could be unutterably cruel, as this scene demonstrates. In our facility in Italy, he was the top trainer, due to the large amount of new programming information that he developed during the war years. This is why in occult groups, he is at times referred to as "the father of modern programming." He discovered that fetuses and very young infants could be programmed, and that in fact, programming done at these impressionable ages when the brain is developing rapidly, is less likely to break down later in life.

Being raised in a cult facility just north of Rome, Italy, the memories I share in this section are some of my earliest ones. I have other memories of Mengele, who I believe, along with Hilde, his blond, blue-eyed assistant, were both dissociative. I believe that they were products of the extreme and cruel programming methods of the early 1900s, when attachment was less understood, and sociopathic personalities were more likely to develop. As far as I know, Hilde, who was raised with him and endured the horrors of their childhood together with him, was the only human being that he trusted, although he did obey orders from those who paid him to program their children, both in Italy and other countries.

Mengele and Hilde were two of my infant trainers, but not my only ones (thank goodness!). I shudder to think of what kind of human being I would have grown up to be if I had not also experienced the kindness at times from the Jesuit fathers who were my primary attachments.

Survival of the Fittest

Mengele liked to use 'survival of the fittest' setups to cull out the weakest babies, and ensure that only the fastest, strongest, most intelligent babies were kept. Fortunately, due to the large numbers of babies that died, this setup was phased out quickly in the Order after his death. By then, I was an adult, and my influence as a trainer, along with that of Mattie, another top trainer, caused this change. We argued successfully that this method was needless, since there were other ways of assessing these qualities. We were also concerned about the long-term impact on the Order's unity, longevity and prosperity, if all our members believed deep in their unconscious minds that their peers were competitors for basic needs, and that the only way for them to survive was for their peers to die.

I can crawl, quickly, now that I am four months old, with soft curly brown hair starting to grow that matches the color of my brown eyes. I am athletic and fast, and perform well in the physical assessments. Today, I am in a small cage with bars. I can see two dozen other similar cages in the room, each containing a baby. I am hungry and thirsty, since I have not been fed for several hours. In the middle of the room are three bottles with formula. I look hungrily at them, I want one! Suddenly, the doors to all of the cages lift simultaneously, and a baby race is on. We all crawl as fast as we can to get to the bottles in the middle of the room.

I, and two of the other fastest babies get there first. Breathing hard, I grab a bottle and start drinking the life-giving, nourishing formula. But two other babies are trying to grab the bottle away from me, they are hungry too. There is a fist grabbing for the bottle, and another baby is climbing onto my back. I have to fight them off, kicking, biting, twisting and turning my back on them, all the while trying to drink the formula as quickly as possible. I am able to successfully keep my bottle and fend off the other hungry babies, using my strong, chubby little legs to kick some away, and get enough formula in me to allay my hunger – and to survive. After a few days of this scenario, the weakest babies are crawling extremely slowly, and I, along with two other of the strongest babies are able to drink a full bottle with barely any resistance from the others.

Mengele walks into the room and picks one of the babies up who is drinking formula, cuddles him, and praises us three, looking at us with a smile. "You are good babies, strong and smart," he tells us. He then goes around the room, and one by one, he hangs a baby from a hook through its gut, in the middle of the room. "This was a weak baby," he says derisively. "This baby didn't try hard enough." He hangs others of the "weak" babies from hooks, and horrified, we three survivors watch. I realize deeply that, in order to survive, I must perform well. Surviving means performing well for Mengele, and I learn quickly to be fast and smart – to find the best way to do something. I don't want to end up on a hook, hanging in the middle of a room.

I am a toddler, several months later, and I hate Mengele, on whom my survival depends. Once again, I am in a cage in a room, with doors that can rise. Next to me is another toddler my age, a little girl. I smile at her, and she smiles at me. In the middle of the room is some food and water, and I already know what will happen.

Suddenly, the doors to our cages lift, and we all run to the middle, trying to fight off each other in a melee that includes mashed faces from tiny fists, kicking, and grabbing. I grab some food, which I eat quickly, grab a drink, and return to my cage.

This happens for two more days, but on this third day, I notice that the little girl in the cage next to me is weakening. I am starting to notice others more at this age, and seeing her look this way bothers me – a lot. When the doors lift, I race to the middle, grab some food, eat a quick bite, then return back to my cage. I then offer some of the food in my little fist to this other toddler. She smiles gratefully at me, but doesn't seem to want to eat; I wonder why, since I was extremely hungry before I ate some of the food. I go over to her cage, and try to put it in her mouth, but she doesn't eat, to my huge distress. I realize now as an adult that she was probably dehydrated and too weak to eat. "Eat, eat, eat" I tell her over and over, but even when I try to put the food in her mouth, she just closes her eyes and falls asleep.

The next morning, she dies and is taken away. As I watch her body being carried out, I cry silently, hiding my tears from Mengele, who would have punished this type of weakness. Fortunately, the fathers were more understanding, and disagreed at times with his methods.

That night, Mattheo, the father I love most of all, notices that I am upset. In my high-pitched little toddler voice, I sob and tell him about the other little girl.

"I am glad that you cared," he says. "But even more glad that you lived. There simply wasn't enough food for all of the babies." While he is trying to promote my acceptance, I can see in his eyes that he is sad and disturbed, too.

"I wanted to share, but she wouldn't eat," I say, crying.

"She was too weak to eat," he says. "But it was good of you to try. And very smart of you to try to find a way to help her."

Mattheo is a rising leader in the Order, and I am glad that he understands. In a few more years, he will be one of the fathers who initiates stopping these survival exercises, with the support of the younger trainers. I love Mattheo and the other fathers, and trust him more than I trust Mengele. But Mengele will never, ever suspect how I feel, because I want to survive, and Mattheo has made it clear that he wants me to live, too.

Many of the infants programmed by Mengele and other trainers in this type of scenario struggled with issues around food all of their lives. When adults, later in life, they hoard food, or gain weight, or become anorexic. Even as a young child, when hosted in my American presentation, I would sneak food and hide it under my pillow. My family teased me relentlessly about this habit, but allowed it, perhaps sensing the deep psychological need to do so.

Mattheo and the other fathers argued successfully to discontinue these methods for several reasons. One was seeing disturbances related to food in the children that survived. But another was that this programming promoted survival at the expense of others, while the

Jesuits wanted their leaders to think of the good of all, when leading teams on missions; they wanted to promote a cohesive working together and bonding with each other that is part of life in the order, and this training went against it. Later generations – those after G7 in the Jesuit Order- would not have to undergo these extreme setups.

Sexual Training

I am just a few weeks old. One of the fathers I love, Father Jerome (who is also a primary trainer) comes into the nursery and stands over my crib. He looks at me lovingly, then takes my diaper off, and rubs me gently with his hand between my legs. It feels nice, but also odd; I feel confused. He continues for a while, and then puts his mouth between my legs.

This happens daily, as part of my early sexual training. I have never known anything else. When these things happen, I am called "Amis". At first, all is gentle and kind, and I learn to accept it as part of being loved by my trainers, as part of the daily routine. After all, this doesn't hurt, unlike some of the other things they do to me.

But after a few weeks, Father Carlotti, another primary trainer comes in. He has a special object in his hand; it is round, small, and not too hard, and he lubricates it and gently inserts it into my rectum. It is uncomfortable, and I wiggle and make a noise of dislike (I have learned not to cry and tantrum in rage already), but he makes a hand signal that means "Be still". The halt and be still commands are among the very first commands I have learned since birth, and so I go limp, as taught, and allow him to continue. After a few seconds more, he stops, and then picks me up and praises me. He tells me, "Amis, what a good baby you are!" with genuine love in his voice, looking me in the eyes with his beautiful amber brown eyes. I wiggle in delight; I have performed well, and he is happy with me, that is all that matters. I am learning that when asked to do things that hurt or make me feel sick inside, I must endure them for the ultimate reward afterwards: love and affection. Father Carlotti holds me against his strong, warm chest for a while, then takes me to one of the female fathers to be nursed.

I have already learned that when I don't perform as asked, I will be punished with even more pain, such as being held upside down by my legs, and whipped with a small but very painful whip. I prefer hugs and praise, so I do what I am asked to do, almost always. I am considered "programmable" and not "difficult" or "resistant" as some babies are, as I learn about when I am older and hear the fathers discussing different babies in the nurseries, categorizing this among other qualities. I also learn when allowed to watch the fathers as an older child that babies who are considered not "programmable" or "too difficult" get slated to be the infant or toddler that dies in various scenarios. But at this young age, I still don't know these things. I work hard to gain the smile and affection from the fathers, which is what they want – for me to perform in order to earn their love and approval.

I am five months old, a vigorous, healthy, happy, active baby. I can already sit up and crawl, and am practicing standing up. I also am able to speak some very simple two-word phrases, and understand my trainers when they speak with me. Father Mattheo, the father I love most of all, comes to my crib. He has some equipment that he hooks me up to, and inwardly I flinch, although outwardly I smile. This is equipment to shock me with, and I am already familiar with it.

He then calls out Amis, and some of the parts that she oversees inside, including Charté, a part that has been previously split from her. As he sexually stimulates Charté with his finger, he also applies mild, but painful, shock at the same time. I have learned not to flinch away from shocks, although internally I am upset at the pairing of what I have associated with "love" with this new pain. I can't help myself; salty tears run down my cheeks, but I don't flail or try to get away.

Mattheo continues doing this for five minutes, telling Charté over and over, "Love is pain. Love is pain. You love pain, it shows love." Afterwards, he stops the shocks, and holds her tenderly, saying, "You are a good baby, and I love you." Charté , while still upset, is glad that this was not a punishment, as shocks can be. He then looks into her young baby eyes, and says, "You must learn to do this. I know it is difficult, and it makes you feel angry, but this is important, and what you are learning is very, very important. I am not doing this to you to punish you, but because I love you. Charté, you are very special for learning to do this and will be able to do great things for me and the other fathers if you learn this." He, and the other fathers, always acknowledge the discomfort and understand the feelings, and discussing them with me and the other parts, even as infants.

Charté is learning to enjoy sadomasochistic sex, and to associate it with feelings of love, arousal, and feeling special and important. Later, she will be dissociated and reorganized into other parts who have only known these feelings, and she will oversee them as a sub-controller within Amis's system. These skills will be used when I am older to help me do missions with individuals who prefer this type of sex, including gathering intelligence or gaining favors. These skills, learned so young, will also help me to survive the extremely painful sexual acts that I will have to endure in some of the homes of the very wealthy around the world. In the order, they do not call us "trafficked", but "skilled"; and our being sent out for various forms of sexual abuse from earliest childhood are considered "missions" for the order.

But deep inside, I feel violated and angry. This is abuse, and my little baby heart and mind know it, even though all of the adults around me treat this as normal, and model it in their own lives. I have learned to hide my anger, but it is there, simmering deep inside. While I love the fathers who rock me, hold me, nurse me and love me, I also hate them with a deep, white-hot hatred.

One thing that the scene above illustrates is that even in infancy, the Jesuit programmers acknowledged how their abuse made me feel. They could tell, by my reactions, the look in my eyes. But then they normalized it within a framework of something that must be done in order to successfully complete missions, as necessary to show my love for them. The Jesuit fathers were masters at manipulating my infant need to attach and maintain a loving bond with them and used it to get me to accept their abuse. The Jesuit programmers understood that a child – even an infant – will do much more for love than in response to any amount of torture, and used this knowledge on me and the other infants I grew up with, just as it was used against them, continuing the cycle of abuse and its normalization generation after generation.

During my own healing, it was a struggle for Amis, Charté and other parts to realize that they had even been abused, since this was "love" to them, the only love they had ever known. They wondered what all the fuss was about when they wanted to continue their activities, even after I left the group, and became aware of their activities and wants that put us in extreme danger. I was quite surprised when Charté came out early in my healing journey, offering to sit on my therapist's lap and give him rough sex; I was also saddened realizing that she had been pushed out by another part inside who wanted to disrupt and distract from what I had been talking about with this therapist. Talking to these parts using logic didn't help. Holding them inside, spending time with them, and showing them other forms of love and experiences that were not sexual helped more.

Bonding to the Fathers

As an infant, each day was broken up into programming, training, comfort, rest, play times and attachment/bonding time on a strictly regimented schedule in the facility nursery. The fathers in the order were experts in child development and were careful to balance training (which was gentle, and filled with praise very early on, with only mild punishments if any for inability to perform in the early weeks) with nurture. They realized that if a child was not given enough nurture, they could develop psychopathic tendencies, would be less controllable (since love is the greatest motivator), and would show other pathologies in psychological or physical development. They knew this because of the failed programming methods used in the early 1900s, when the children were not given enough nurturing and failed to attach to a loving adult caregiver: many had to be "put down" later as they developed severe psychopathic tendencies, to the point of killing the trainers that they did not love, without a twinge of regret.

Oh, how carefully the fathers monitored and doled out "love" to us infants, and we came to look expectantly for that special time each day with the "fathers we loved". Each infant had three primary fathers they bonded with, along with nine others who were also important to their emotional development and training. I loved three special fathers the most: Father Mattheo, Father Jerome, and Father Carlotti. I was also very closely bonded to Father John, an older female trainer, and Father Daniel, a female trainer who also nursed me and filled the "mother" role in my life. Females upon becoming a Jesuit father took on male names, so this was considered normal in the Order. The Jesuits always had several trainers that bonded closely to each infant, since they realized that otherwise, if an infant bonded to only one individual and that individual died, the baby or child would be at a huge risk for failure to thrive, or would be basically un-programmable. They learned this, also, from the failures of the early 1900s, when some children bonded to only one primary trainer, who died. Data was collected on these children, and they kept it in their huge library of training materials and information, as well as coded into a huge computer database that could be accessed with a simple series of codes and voice commands for those authorized to do so.

So I, and the other infants I was raised with, bonded to the fathers we loved. But the fathers I loved also tortured me and the other babies. Infancy and childhood was a strange mix of torture and being held and rocked lovingly; being nursed by the same individual who later sexually abused me.

I am just a few months old, and angry about the pain the fathers inflict upon me. I feel sullen. While I have been trained to look up and smile when the fathers come into the nursery, today, I turn away. I turn my back on these men and women who bring me daily pain. It is Father Carlotti who comes by my crib, and sees my angry turning away.

"You cannot act this way," he tells me curtly in Italian. "You are being a bad baby to act this way, and must be punished."

He then goes and gets a couple of wrist holders and straps. He places the wrist holders around my chubby wrists, and then as punishment hangs me by my arms from the side of my crib. This hurts terribly, I feel as if my small arms which do not yet have the muscles and ligaments to take this, are being wrenched out of their sockets. The muscles burn as they are stretched. My arms do pull out of their sockets and I scream in pain.

Carlotti repeats, "This is what happens to bad babies who turn away, and don't turn and hold their arms up." He holds me with one hand, releasing my wrists with his other, and assesses me for the extent of the physical damage. He takes me to a healing room, and uses technology to put the arms back into their shoulder sockets, and to heal the joints and ligaments that have been so painfully stretched.

"Don't do this again," he warns. I don't.

I came to hate and fear that phrase, "bad baby", used by Mengele and the fathers, as something to avoid at all costs. "Bad babies" cried, turned away from, and kicked at their programmers, and did not greet them with an unfailing smile. "Bad babies" were allowed one or two chances, but after that," bad babies" were hung on hooks from the nursery ceiling until they died, or were seen in "hell" later that day, being whipped to death by "demons" (children in costumes). We all learned to be "good babies": compliant and programmable, and never to show how we really felt about how we were being treated. We were taught to send that anger down into an "anger pit" filled with anger-holding parts inside; this rage would then be directed at other objects, such as Christians, outsiders, and most importantly, ourselves.

This inability to show my feelings at the person who caused them fostered intense dissociation which the fathers had already carefully conditioned me to rely on while in the womb and during the early weeks after birth. I already had the structure in place to 'dissociate away' into designated parts the angry feelings out of my fear of punishment for "bad babies" and to focus on performing well and being a "good baby".

In the memory above, I also mention the healing rooms. The programming facility had state-of-the-art healing technologies that even over sixty years ago were far ahead of what is commercially available to healthcare providers currently. There were vats filled with saline and electrolyte/mineral solutions of various types, with various types of frequencies to promote healing, and even artificial skin that when lit with a red light would help new skin to grow rapidly. Because of the ongoing, physical abuse, these technologies were necessary to prevent permanent scarring or disability for the children being programmed, as well as older children and adults who might come back injured from dangerous or strenuous missions, or who might be accidentally injured during training and military exercises.

The Drawer

I am a few months old, and I am upset. Father Jerome is taking out the wires and electrodes that I have come to hate; wires and electrodes that cause sharp, biting pain with the electric shocks that they conduct. I don't want this! When he tries to put the electrodes on me, I kick and squirm and wiggle away, struggling to avoid these stinging wires being placed on me.

"This type of behavior can't be allowed. Be still!" he commands sternly.

But I am not still. I disobey him, for I am still very small, and do not know yet what can be done to ensure compliance. His command instills less fear in me than the fear that the memory of shocks that sting like bees, shocks that cause terrible, burning pain. I don't want to be hurt, so I continue to resist, arching my back in protest and screaming.

Father Jerome stops, then takes a key hanging around his neck, and with it, opens a small drawer. This drawer has padding on the bottom and sides. He picks me up, saying, "You will experience utter darkness, the hell reserved for disobedience such as this." He then places me into the drawer, and slides it shut it with a loud "click".

It is utterly dark and soundless in this drawer. I can breathe, but there is no light, no noise, nothing. It is quiet, and I am afraid. I wait to see what will happen.

Time passes, and I am frightened and hungry. I cry and cry with ever louder wails, but no one hears. My diaper is wet and filled with stool, and I am afraid. No one can see or hear me in this place; no one is there to take care of me. I am a little baby, and I know that I will die if no one takes care of me. I depend on the adults around me for everything. And now, there is...nothing. Just black darkness. I am terrified.

Time passes, where I alternate between loud screams of terror, and soft whimpers. Finally, I am too exhausted to cry any longer. I fall asleep.

I am very sleepy; maybe I will never wake up. I am starting to feel very far away and strange, as if my body is getting smaller and further away. Maybe this is what dying is like. It feels like a long time has passed, and I am resigned to being here forever, and dying.

Suddenly, I hear the drawer slide open. There is a light, much too bright for my eyes which have been in complete darkness for so long, even though it is just the dim light that is on in the nursery at night.

Father Jerome is there, and I am frantic, desperate for him to take me out of this terrible, terrible box. "Will you obey me now?" he asks, looking me in the eyes. He sees the terror and pleading in them, and lifts me out of the box of terror, of abandonment.

He holds me for awhile, close to his chest, then gives me part of a bottle. I drink, but keep looking at his eyes the whole times, frantic for him to respond to my frantic terror and need for him to not leave me alone. Later, he takes me into a white room with a rocking chair, and rocks me for a period of time. Finally, I relax and rest awhile.

The next morning, Father Jerome returns, comes to my crib, and tries to put the electrodes on me. I do not struggle or resist this time.

These drawers are reserved as punishment for resisting being programmed, and being placed in one was one of the cruelest tortures that I experienced as an infant. The sense of utter abandonment and terror was overwhelming, but it also ensured compliance in an infant that comes to realize that emotional survival depends upon obedience to what the trainers demand, no matter how difficult.

Learning to Crawl Towards Colored Lights

I am a baby, able to crawl but not able to do much else, yet. After all, I am only three months old. I am on the smooth floor of one of the programming labs. I have been told to wait. Suddenly, I hear six notes played in a specific sequence. Simultaneously, a code is flashed in front of me on a large overhead screen: it is a black and white pattern in a specific configuration meant to bring out a specific part. I have already learned to bring the correct parts out when different tones and patterns are shown to me during the previous first few weeks of life, and have become quite good at it, to the pleased smiles and "good girl!" comments from the fathers I love. This ability to make them so happy makes me coo and wiggle with joy.

Now, a part loyal to the Jesuit Order is out, and a green light, about the size of a traffic light, shines down the smooth tunnel I am crawling through as I crawl towards this light. The tunnel is bathed in the green light, as Cerachnid-1, a cult-loyal presenter, is learning that green is her color, just as the tone sequence and pattern are hers. This task is fun, and when Cerachnid reaches the light, she is given a piece of soft fruit as a special treat by Father Jerome, a man in his early 20s who already has white hair that looks beautiful with his clear blue eyes.

"Cerachnid, you did well," he tells her. Jerome then picks me up in his strong arms and cuddles me against the soft folds of his lab uniform. "Cerachnid, you are so special for being able to do this," he says, and Cerachnid wiggles with delight at the praise in his voice. "I love you," Jerome tells her. "I am glad that you had fun doing this." During this early part of training, there are lots of rewards and hugs when Cerachnid and other parts perform well, doing simple tasks such as recognizing cues to come out; recognizing their special colors, and obeying the trainers.

Punishments will come later on after this first, primary belief is instilled deeply: obedience to cues brings feelings of love, security, joy, and is even "fun".

It is a month later. Cerachnid has been performing very well, but now something very important happens to her. Cerachnid undergoes extremely severe pain, being told ahead what will happen. The fathers always tell parts when pain is going to happen, they never hide this fact.

Cerachnid cannot endure this pain, and her mind starts dissociating from it, creating new little babies from herself. These new parts are quickly given names as each comes out; a code specific to them is flashed on the screen above her, and these new cult loyal parts split from Cerachnid become the system parts that she will oversee and eventually learn to control.

"You must keep these parts safe, Cerachnid," Father Jerome tells her. She understands what "safe" means; it means making sure that they obey and believe everything they are told. Her job is make sure that they obey and believe; this is the only "safe" that she and others inside have experienced.

Cerachnid will eventually learn to forget that these other parts originally came from her, and instead, will see herself as protecting them from "further harm" (going through the agonizing pain, pain that made her feel as if she was dying, of her original splitting memory). She is told that she can only keep them "safe" by ensuring that they are always "good" by being obedient to programming cues and commands. Her desire to protect these parts dissociated from herself from experiencing further pain and trauma actually reflects the deep, instinctive self-love that all babies have for themselves, which the programmers are counting upon as they cause her and other primary controller parts to dissociate and then re-organize into subsidiary, system parts.

It is several weeks later, and I am four and a half months old. Cerachnid is taken to a special room in the programming lab. There is a huge tree pattern laid out on the floor, with a trunk, roots, branches and leaves. She has already met "Gnossis" (the tree of knowledge), a woman dressed in a tree costume, who visited her crib numerous times over the past few months, and explained to her who she is. Cerachnid now sees the face of this woman embedded in the center of the tree, inlaid with the bark, and wiggles with recognition.

"Cerachnid, it is time for you to learn where you live on the tree," the soft, beautiful voice says. "Come to your place." At that moment, a special pattern (Cerachnid's code), a small green light and the musical sequence play on a specific branch, close to the trunk.

Cerachnid is guided by the trainer to this spot, and she sits.

"This is where you will live," says the soft voice of the tree. "This is your special place where you can feel safe; if you leave your special place, you and those you protect and help – your system – will be unsafe". The trainer then comes and hugs Cerachnid, and gives her a soft, sweet rusk to suck on. They spend time in peaceful activity, while one limb of the tree slowly strokes Cerachnid's back and the trainer murmurs loving words to her. After a few minutes, the trainer calls out another part whose job is to not remember the programming session, Cerachnid goes back in, and the trainer picks me up and carries me out of the lab. I have no memory of what happened inside the lab; only Cerachnid will remember learning her place on the tree.

This gentle, loving scene is repeated numerous times over the next few weeks for Cerachnid and other system controllers, until each one understands their "place" on the tree; my system controllers are major branches, with their system parts the outlying twigs, and programs (leaves) that branch out from them.

It is not until this program, and the deep feeling of love and safety for going to the correct place on the tree, and remaining there, is instilled, that the punishments for leaving the designated place or disobedience are installed. For the rest of her life, Cerachnid will always seek to return to that initial sense of peace, safety and being loved that underpinned her programming. And for her, this means complete, unquestioning obedience and belief in what her trainers tell her.

The above memory illustrates how the Jesuit trainers use a combination of concrete, physical structures and activities for their training of infants and young children, combined with rewards and punishments to ensure that expected behaviors will be instilled. But this, like all programming, will often rest upon an earlier, primary memory, of a time when the controller was loved and felt safe; in essence, a "resting place" that the controller will always try to return to whenever possible. The trainers provide a framework for the only way this feeling of security and attachment can be attained: being programmable, and obedient to the programs being installed by the trainers.

Early Training and Assessment

I love the other infants I am living with in the large nursery filled with cribs. We are fed bottles of milk at the same time, and later sit at a short table and eat together as we become able to sit up. During free time, we play together. Most of all, we learn to do things together.

I am a year old. I and the other infants my age are being told to sit in groups of four at small child-sized tables with colored blocks.

"I want you all to build a tower with all blue blocks on the bottom, all red in the row above, and then all yellow blocks at the top. I want you to do this together when you hear the bell ring," Mattie is telling us. She is one of the top 11-year-olds in programming. Behind her is Father Timothy, her mentor. She enjoys working with us babies, and he is watching her as well as us.

Timothy and Mattie go from table to table, giving each the same instructions. In a bit, a bell rings and we start. This is fun, and I laugh as the other one-year-olds and I do this simple task. We create a small tower of blocks as instructed.

"Good, very good," Mattie praises us. I like her; she is warm and caring and tries to praise us whenever we do well. The other toddlers and I grin at each other. As we look around the room, we see that the other toddlers are finishing up, too.

"You all did really well," Timothy says. "You can have lunch now."

Lunch is brought in, and we enjoy the soft fruit, vegetables and liver. The food is always, always very healthy and tasty, and because we are so physically active, all of us are hungry. The food doesn't last long.

There are other small group activities given over the next few months: figuring out how to share four apples among twelve of us, or how to climb a wall that is too high to simply put a leg over. As we do these things, and learn to work as a team, the fathers praise us, and give us extra "free time" to simply play with each other. Free time is a precious commodity in this highly structured environment, and we all decide to perform well to gain as much free time as possible, in order to simply be toddlers.

This pattern will continue throughout my life. When my class did well, or I am part of a mission team that does well, we can sometimes choose our reward, and we choose time off. The programmers and facility heads knew that we valued most of all the times when we could simply be human beings without expectations of performance. They allowed for this, but it had to be earned.

Because of genetic engineering for intelligence, all the babies in the nursery had high IQs, and we all achieved behavioral milestones very early. Most of us were toddling by six to seven months of age on plump but muscular baby legs, and we were starting to talk as well, in high-pitched baby voices. We understand what those around us are saying, although we are still unable to follow complex, abstract discussions, and can only respond in simple phrases.

During the early years, we are assessed and sorted according to leadership gifts, intelligence, strength and creativity, as well as other qualities, into groups of similar abilities. These sortings are held loosely during the first three years of life, with ongoing testing and assessments throughout life. The activities described here function not only to teach the children skills, but also enable the fathers to assess the children. But by age six, we will be sorted into classes of 12 of similar abilities for further training and education at the specialized 'school' run by the Order. As children, we attend this school from six until twelve years old. I recall my cohort as having four classes of 12 children.

Angel in the Labs

I am four months old. Like the other infants in the nursery, I am sleeping soundly. It is the middle of the night, and we have had a busy day learning new tasks and doing all the things that little babies growing up in a programming facility do. It is quiet, the lights are down, and the darkened room is silent except for the occasional rustle of a baby moving a bit on soft sheets.

Suddenly, something wakes me up. I look around and see a figure walking through the nursery. This figure looks like one of the immortals, but something about it is very different. The robes are soft, almost transparent, and shine with a soft light. This being has golden hair and a kind face. I watch as it stops by a crib and places its hand on a baby's head. The baby wakes up and smiles at the being.

As it walks nearer to my crib, I see white wings folded behind him. I feel that this is a male being, without being sure why. As it gets closer and closer, placing his hand softly on each baby's head, the babies smile. Some sit up and lean towards him, reaching after him as he goes to another crib. Finally, he comes to my crib. I smile at him, and his golden eyes look at me with tenderness and love. He places his hand on my head, as if in benediction, and suddenly I feel something I have never felt before. I feel peace, utter peace, and safety. I want this feeling to go on forever. This being does not smell like the other immortals who visit, but instead, seems to bring the smell of a beautiful breeze from somewhere else that floats around him. This smell is wonderful, and I want him to stay with me. But the being keeps going until the babies in the nursery have all had a hand placed on them. Then, the being silently, quietly disappears.

After the being is gone, several fathers come into the lab. Father Mattheo comes to my crib. "You should not have let that malak — that messenger from the enemy — touch you," he says. His voice is angry, I have no idea what I did wrong. Don't beings come at night all the time? Why shouldn't I let him touch me? Don't all the immortals touch me? I think all of these things, but cannot speak them yet. "That was one of the liar's messengers; that was not an immortal," Mattheo says. He must have seen the being come into the nursery. But it is not until I am much older that I learn that he and the other fathers could not stop it. They had to wait until it left.

I feel bewildered. This being was kind, and the peace and love I felt coming from its touch was even better than the words and cake that the "immortals" were bringing me at night. How could a being this nice be an "enemy"?

The next morning, Father Mattheo shows me a depiction of an angel, and shocks me over and over as he shows it to me, telling me, "These are the enemy. Send them away if they come to you." I understand that he wants me to hate this gentle visitor in the night and start to associate him with the shocks. The shocks are my enemy, but my baby brain thinks they are caused by the picture of the angel that I am being shown.

Learning to Stay on the Path

I am 18 months old, and my hand is being held by an adult dressed in a costume to represent Gnossis, the Tree of the Knowledge of Good and Evil. She has a crown of leafy branches on her head, and her arms have numerous leafy branches that appear to sprout out of them; even her fingers look like small twigs. Her middle is covered by rough looking "bark", and her feet are covered with what appeared to be several layers of roots. Her voice is calm, patient, and melodious as she takes me by the hand, and leads me down a pathway that is outlined with wide, white brick pavers.

"You must always, always stay on the path, and never depart," she instructs me. "Only by staying on the path of righteousness and knowledge can you ascend and reach the celestial heights. Otherwise, you will descend into mortality and suffer the torments of the wicked – those who choose the flesh over immortality." As she leads me, the pavers under our feet light up with a soft, diffuse glow; it seems wonderful and magical to me as a toddler. "If you follow the path, your way will be lighted with increasing knowledge," she assures me. When we come to the end of this part of the path, it divides, and we go to the right. We then rest on a small bench, and she gives me a sweet treat as a reward for being such a good child and following the path with her so well.

These walks along the path continue at intervals over the next few months. I learn exactly where to go and am warned where not to go each time by one of the three trees who lead me along this path: Althea, the tree of life; Gnossis, the tree of knowledge (of good and evil); and the Servant tree. These paths actually represent following my internal programming, which I have been told is the path to immortality. But at this young age, my main concern right now is to always stay on the path. I have been told that dreadful things will happen if I fail to, and I don't want these sweet, caring trees to become angry with me.

After another month, when I am almost two years old, Althea starts me on the path, and then smiling, she says, "You know the way, child. Remember to always stay on it, and all will be well." She then leaves me, and I start to follow the path. But along the way, I see to the side of the path some chocolate treats on a table, just a few feet off of the path. I start to go past, but then pause, and look longingly at the treat. I love chocolates, and want one very much. I think *Maybe no one will know if I go off for just a few seconds, grab a treat, then go back on the path.*

I step off of the path, and suddenly the room grows dark, a cold wind blows, and I feel terrible, hot, sharp electric shocks beneath my feet that cause me to cry out in pain. I hear shrieks and screams, and demonic looking figures lurking in the now completely darkened room start coming towards me; I can hear their snarls and hisses, and back away.

I can't find the path! It is hidden in this dark place, and I am terrified. I scream aloud, asking Althea to help, and suddenly I see a soft glow in the distance that comes closer. It is Althea, and she looks very sad and concerned.

"Why did you go off the path, child?" she asks with great sorrow. Her beautiful crystal clear blue eyes are filled with tears.

Terrified, I look at her, then stutter, "I...I...I w-w-wanted chocolate..." Tears are streaming down my face, and I feel deeply ashamed and guilty about my disobedience.

She sighs. "You let your mortal flesh, your mortal desires take over, instead of staying on the path," she says sternly. "Don't you realize that I warned you to stay on for your own good? Staying on the path is the only path to safety."

I realize that she is right, because even taking a small step off the path brought disaster in the form of extreme pain and terror.

"Will you stay on the path, and not go off again?" she asks.

"Y-y-yes," I say, having no desire to experience the terrors and pain of mortality and descending again. It hurt, badly. Althea then smiles, and her clear blue eyes light up with joy.

"Good." She stoops down to eye level, looks me in the eyes, and says, "I trust you to desire immortality more than to gratify your flesh." She then leaves me on a portion of the path near where I started out. I walk along the path for a time, and suddenly see candies in a bowl on the side of the path, just out of reach. But this time, I do not step off the path, a path which represents my staying within the prescribed programming for my system, of which I am a controller. Instead, this time, I ignore the candy and continue on, until I am greeted by a delighted Althea who praises me warmly.

"You are learning not to give in to the flesh, and to desire immortality," she says in loving tones. "You are doing well, indeed." She then takes me into her arms (I am still quite small) and ascends the celestial stairway – a golden stairway that goes up and up towards the ceiling, taking me to the celestial realms – another part of the programming lab up above that has fluffy clouds to walk on and beautiful, sparkly stars all around on the walls. Together, Althea and I enjoy a wonderful treat of cream cake. The other celestials there praise me and tell me how glad they are that I am learning to overcome my mortal flesh.

While I was too young at the time to fully understand why I had to stay on the path, I came to understand over time that the path was my programming, and that stepping off of it, even a little bit, would bring pain and terror. During these initial early years of programming, the costumed adults and children who represent celestial beings such as the trees are loving, kind and instill the belief that these beings – who are also internalized, or become part of my internal mental landscape, as important controllers – want only what is best for the child and their systems.

This makes the very young child want to obey them, want to make them happy, which is a much stronger underpinning for obedience than simply terror. Even as an adult, the young system parts and controllers will still want to obey their internal primary controllers, believing that they want what is best and safest for their survival. This makes the programming even more difficult to break later in life, than if a simple desire to avoid punishment was used. An analogy that can be used – although imperfect – is the difference between a child who is abused and maltreated growing up, without any display of love to the child, and a child who has experiences of being deeply loved and attached to a parent who often sorrowfully takes off a belt and thrashes them until they are covered with black and blue stripes from neck to ankle, saying "This is for your own good." Both children have experienced severe abuse, but the latter child, who believes the parent genuinely cares for them, may find it more difficult to define their treatment as "abuse" and will be more likely to internalize their parent's beliefs.

Failure to Thrive

There was only one time when the constant demand to perform was relaxed.

I am about seven months old. I have stopped eating and I am beginning to lose weight. I turn my head away, even with threats from the trainers. I simply don't care, even if they kill me.

I am feeling utter, complete despair. Somewhere in the depths of my developing mind is a dawning understanding that my life is one of frequent abuse, paired with the demand to perform, and then perform still harder, and do things repugnant to me even as a baby. I have no control, and this is to be my life, and this knowledge overwhelms me. I want choice, I desperately want a choice, and it is not allowed. So, I make the only choice that I can make. I choose to die and fail to thrive.

In later years, as a trainer myself, I saw this phenomenon many times in infants. In fact, it was expected at some point in infants who are pushed to the limit of their emotional, physical and spiritual endurance. Most survived, but some did end up dying. The threat of death is real.

As soon as the symptoms occur, a change is made in my routine. The programming stops. Mattheo, Jerome and Carlotti come, and hold me and rock me in the rocking chair near my crib. "I love you," Mattheo whispers. "Don't die, little one; I would feel so sad." He believes what he is telling me, and I feel his words. But I still cannot eat. The despair is too deep.

Jerome and Carlotti also come and hold me and talk to me. My twin siblings – I am part of a triplet set, which is what the Jesuits raise instead of twins- Daniel (Danny) and Elizabeth (Lizzy), who I love and am bonded to, are placed in my crib with me. This is unheard of, but the fathers are desperate. I am losing more weight and have pale skin and dull eyes. Danny coos to me, and holds a small bottle out to me, trying to get me to eat a little and to play with him. I smile, just a little, at this brother who I love so much. His love reaches me, and very hesitantly, I pick up the bottle and take a tiny sip. Lizzie, my other twin, looks at my face and pats it with her little baby hands. She tries to make me smile by blowing loud raspberries at me. I smile weakly at her.

Soon, one of the female fathers comes over to my crib, picks me up, and nurses me in the rocking chair nearby. She is my "birth mother," not the real one, of course, but the one my parts have bonded to after the death of the real one. She whispers to me, "I love you, I love you," over and over, her light brown hair falling softly forward as she looks me in the eyes with her grey eyes filled with tenderness. I nurse a bit and fall asleep. I am exhausted with the exhaustion of deep depression, even at this young age. But the rocking is soothing, and for this time, being treated almost like a real baby, and less like a circus performer, something in me unwinds a bit. Maybe there are good things in life, too.

The next day, two of the fathers walk by. I hear them discussing Danny, Lizzie and me. "If she doesn't make the decision to live, we will have to put the other two to death, too," I hear them say. I am horrified. Even if I don't want to live, I want my little brother and sister to live. Danny and Lizzie, sitting in the crib next to me, are looking at me with big, sad brown eyes. I realize that they, too, have overheard the fathers discussing us. A small tear falls down Dannie's cheek; he wants to live, I can feel it as strongly as if he has spoken to me. His brown curls tremble slightly as he leans over and gives me a little kiss on my cheek.

I take the bottle that is lying in my crib, and start drinking from it. I have decided to live, to save my little brother and sister, whose lives I now realize depend on mine. As I drink the formula, Dannie and Lizzie smile with baby joy, and Lizzie claps her little hands with a soft "pat, pat" noise.

It is not until years later that I realize that this conversation by the fathers was meant to be overheard; it was no accident. They wanted me to believe that my siblings would die if I died, to motivate me. But as an infant, I had no way of realizing that they were using my love for others against me.

I survive, I start gaining back the weight that I had lost. After a few more days of rest, I am put back into the daily routine, but am carefully monitored for any further signs of failing to thrive.

And the bonding continues with the fathers, these fathers who caused me to want to die with their abuse, their torture, their demands. Each day, usually at the end of the day, Mattheo comes in to spend special time with me, for 15 to 30 minutes each day. He holds me and talks to me with loving words. "You are such a beautiful daughter," he tells me as he rocks and comforts me. "I love you," he says as he holds me close to his warm chest, treating me the way a father would treat their beloved baby. "I'm so proud of you; you are wonderful," he says at the end of a long, hard day of learning and performing.

I look forward to this special time with great eagerness. This is what makes all the hard work, the terrible abuse, the punishments and rewards, all worth it: to earn the love of this human being that I adore so much. I will do anything for him, even live.

Infants in the Jesuit nurseries are allowed to bond deeply with both the fathers, and their genetic triplets; these babies are allowed extra time together in simple play. But the fathers are masters at manipulating these love bonds in order to gain the behaviors they want. When I first had this memory, I felt enraged. Enraged that my very ability to love others, to care, was used so callously against me. Enraged that even the choice to die and escape as a baby was wrested away from me, due to my inability to allow my siblings to die. This desire to rescue others will be used again and again throughout the rest of my life to control me, and it is a heavy weight to bear indeed, until I learn that no human being can truly "rescue" another; that there is only one who can rescue without manipulation or demands, and that is Jesus.

Chapter 2: Early Spiritual Training

Meeting the Immortals

I am only a few weeks old, and I am lying in my crib. Suddenly, two beautiful women in soft, glowing silvery dresses and two men in glowing robes of the same color come and stand by my bed. I am enthralled at these beautiful people who walk softly and talk with melodious voices. They lean over my crib and speak.

"Child, we are the immortals," they say in unison. Their voices are sweet and musical, and sound like those of angels. "Because you are blessed, we have chosen to visit you. You are fortunate indeed." I grin a toothless baby grin and wiggle my arms and legs happily. These people seem nice, and they seem to like me.

"My name is Calexa" says the woman with beautiful silvery hair, as she picks me up and holds me tenderly. She holds me upright so that I can clearly see the other woman, whose soft golden brown hair seems to be waving about her face in the nearly darkened room.

"My name is Althea, and I bring wisdom to those who seek me," the brown-haired woman says. On her dress is a golden rune, a picture of a tree. She continues, "You will grow to love me, as I already love you, chosen one."

Then a man with golden hair and beautiful blue eyes approaches me next. "I am Paltheus, and will teach you how to do difficult things; but you will grow strong and beautiful as a result. I want you to be strong, and to one day join us where we live." He takes me from Calexa and cuddles me gently in his strong arms. I feel warm and secure against his chest, as I smell his wonderful smell; he smells like roses and lavender and sweet things. These immortals are wonderful people.

Baltheus is the next "immortal" to talk to me. He has silver-white hair and grey eyes that look suspiciously like those of Mattheo, my primary trainer. "If you learn to love me as I love you and do all that I and my mortal representatives tell you to do, then I will give you the gift of seeing what is to come in the future, and to look into and see what is in men's hearts." I am still too young to fully understand all of this, but I recognize his kind tone and the loving way he holds and rocks me. I am filled with joy at the attention they are giving me.

"We will come again soon," these beautiful people say as they leave, and just as they promised, they do visit again.

Several times a week, they and other fathers dressed as "immortals" visit me in the nursery. During each visit, they teach me about who they are, and what abilities they can give me. This is an important part of my spiritual training. I also see them visit the other babies in the nursery and tell them the same or similar things. I feel I must be a lucky baby indeed to be visited by such loving, beautiful people – or "immortals", the "divine" as I am learning to call them. My only confusion is that they feel and smell like real people to me, in spite of their words; they actually smell like some of the fathers I know. I wonder why, but go back to sleep, dreaming about being held and loved by these people in silvery soft robes.

The Jesuit fathers use very concrete setups to teach infants and young children their spiritual beliefs, which include ascending towards immortality, or else descending towards mortality (and pain). An infant and young child will willingly believe what they are taught at this age, especially if their lessons are conveyed through concrete experiences like the 'role-playing' and 'acting' by the fathers and older children in costumes, as depicted in this account.

Celestial Heaven

A few weeks later, I and the other babies in my nursery are awakened in the middle of the night by the soft tread of the "immortals" who walk into our room on silver slippers. I am picked up and carried by an "immortal", Charydon, a man with beautiful long white hair and green eyes, He says, "I am going to take you to a very special place – the place where I live. I want you to see what the celestial realms look like. This is where you can one day live if you are very, very good." I already know that "good" means being obedient and doing all that the programmers tell me; the "immortals" have already been telling me that my programmers are the "mortal representatives" of the "immortals" and that obeying them is the same as obeying an "immortal".

Charydon carries me in his strong, muscular arms and walks up a beautiful golden spiral staircase that is strung with glittering stars and what looks like planets along the darkened areas beside it. Up, up we go, until finally, he is walking on what looks like soft, puffy white clouds with glitter and rainbow lights everywhere. It is beautiful, and I hear lovely singing from far away, by voices that sound like angels. It is not until I am much older that I will learn that these voices are actually older children singing, with their voices piped in. As a little baby, I have no idea that as I get older, when I am eleven or twelve years old, I will also be singing songs of the 'celestial realm' for new groups of babies.

I look everywhere about me. Charydon holds me carefully upright in his arms so that I can see as much as possible. I see beautiful, ethereal figures with wings flitting by in the background. The smell is wonderful, like flowers and perfume and rose candy all at once.

"Little one, would you like to try some celestial food?" Charydon asks in a loving, gentle voice. I look at him wonderingly, and he places a bit of a very soft, sweet substance on my tongue; it tastes like whipped cream and fruit together, and the taste is wonderful. "This is the food of the gods," he explains, "and those who ascend and overcome their mortality are able to come here and enjoy it." I think it is wonderful, that this whole place is absolutely wonderful. I want to be able to come here and eat things like this, so I decide to ascend as soon as possible.

After a while, Charydon's voice becomes tinged with sorrow. "We must now descend back to the mortal realms," he explains, with a *pathos* that makes me realize that he, too, hates to leave this wonderful place. He looks into my eyes and smiles, and says, "But if you are very good, and I know you will be, we will come back here soon." I smile back, and he gently carries me back down the golden stairs, down past the stars, as we descend. Finally, we are at the bottom, and he carries me back into the nursery and gently lays me in my crib.

I am so excited from this experience that it takes me a while to settle back into sleep. But the fathers and Mengele start training the next day several hours later than normal. It is as if they, too, understand how important it is to spend time with the immortals, and are willing to change the daily routine to allow for this.

I remember that Charydon, Althea and the other immortals told me that my trainers were their mortal representatives, and how important it is to always obey them if I want to "ascend" and visit the celestial realms again. I am very obedient for the next few days, and as promised, another immortal, Baltheus, comes and visits me a few nights later. He also helps me to "ascend" the beautiful staircase to visit the celestial realms. They are teaching me that I need the help of an immortal to visit this spiritual place as they must carry me there. This lays the foundation, for me to later in life allow the demonic to 'carry me' or 'help me to ascend' into the 'celestial realms'.

These visits occur regularly during my first two years of life. As a toddler, I toddle around the clouds, which feel like soft puffs of cotton beneath my slippered feet. I am given wonderful cake to eat and learn from these beautiful beings many of the rules of the immortals and how to enter these realms. I am being inculcated in the belief system that underlies all of the programming, all of the rituals, all of the hard work being done by the Order: the desire to allow the immortals to visit earth, and to ascend in order to be with them in the celestial realms.

I am much too young to recognize that these immortals are adults dressed in costumes or that the stairway is part of a programming lab. Nor am I yet able to recognize that the celestial realms are a programming studio with special props. I will only learn this years later. By that time, however, I believe utterly in the celestials. I have also by that time become completely indoctrinated with my mentors' teaching that the celestial programming studio is a necessary teaching tool for babies too young to grasp the spiritual realities of the immortals and am blind to the fact that it is nothing but trickery to manipulate the babies into obedience to satanic agendas.

Again, this is an example of the extremely elaborate setups that are used to indoctrinate the very young infants with a belief in the immortals – this belief that underpins the Jesuit Order in its occult side. Readers may wonder how on earth setups this elaborate are possible. But the Jesuits have lots of money that comes from their human trafficking and intelligence work as well as other dark operations. With billions of dollars at their disposal, and state-of-the-art technology that is many years ahead of current technologies, they have had no trouble constructing advanced programming facilities. They have facilities in numerous countries with the largest and best-funded ones being in Italy.

The older children and adults enjoy dressing up in costumes, and everyone loves the celestial scenes, hoping to be chosen to take the young babies and toddlers up the golden studio stairs, and watch their delight in the beauty and sweet treats. While the fathers, due to their own dissociation, mind control, and erroneous beliefs, feel that these young children must be abused during programming, the truth is that everyone feels a sense of relief when they are scheduled to participate in a happy training setup such as described above. The fathers view the abusive programming as a "necessary thing" but still dislike it, in spite of a lifetime of training to normalize it.

Typically, immediately after the older children or adults put costumes on for particular setups, other programmers who are overseeing that particular setup will first call up the appropriate parts in those individuals. For instance, in the setup described here where they will play 'immortals', 'angels' and other roles, parts who have been programmed to be 'immortals' and so on will be the ones called up. This means that when the adults and children participate in these indoctrination scenarios through these parts, they are not aware that they are 'acting' out roles in a studio but are personally convinced that they are taking a baby to the celestial realms, or that they are angels singing in the realms. Their utter conviction is part of what causes the scenarios to feel absolutely authentic to the babies. Besides helping to program the babies, using the programmed parts of other cult members serves to reinforce that programming of these cult members themselves, as their internal parts are called out to present, and act out their roles in those programming studios under the programmers' supervision.

Mortal Hell

It is a few weeks after Althea and the other immortals last visited me. I am awakened in the middle of the night by a dark and malevolent being. Years later, I will learn that this is an older child dressed in a costume, but in the darkened nursery, this creature looks and sounds terrifying, with long, dark claws, long sharp fangs, red glowing eyes, and a twisted, dark shape.

"You were bad today, and you are coming with me," it croaks in a demonic voice, with sibilant hissing. Now, I am really scared. I wonder what I could have possibly done that got the attention of this...thing... Obviously, I must have broken some unwritten, not understood rule.

The creature picks me up roughly, its claws biting into my tiny arm as it does so. It carries me out of the nursery. I am struggling hard to free myself from its grasp, but to no avail. This creature takes me into a room with a large, black, cavernous hole in the middle. There are steps going down into the dark, scary looking steps. I struggle even harder, but I am held in its iron grip.

"We are going to descend," the creature croaks, and it carries me down, down, down into a place where the air smells smoky, and there are red flames flickering on the walls. I see black poles that fill this room. Men and women are tied to them by chains. "Demons" (as usual, the older cult children dressed in costumes) are whipping them with long whips with bits of bone attached. The men and women are screaming in tortured pain.

"Because you were disobedient, you will join the other mortals who chose to give in to their flesh, and to descend. They caused themselves to come here because they did not listen to the wise counsel of the immortals," the demonic actor hisses in my ear.

I begin crying, but the dark creature doesn't care. He ties me to a pole that has a small stand to hold me, almost like an infant seat, since I am too young to stand yet. The small chain bites into my little arms and chest.

The creature then takes out a small whip and lashes my tiny arms and legs. While there is no real injury, the lashes sting sharply and add to my terror. I am now screaming at the top of my lungs.

Suddenly, Father Mattheo appears, dressed in the silvery robes of an immortal. "Do you promise to always obey me, and to try to never give in to your mortal desires again; to try and listen to the wisdom of the immortals?" he asks.

I look at him with huge eyes, and raise my right fist, the sign language I have learned for "yes", since I have forgotten in my terror how to speak.

Father Mattheo then turns to the "demon" and says, "Let her loose, I will vouch for her."

The twisted, grimacing, dark creature reluctantly looses the tiny jangly chains that hold me in place, and Mattheo picks me up and soothes me, in spite of the fact that I have had a loose bowel movement due to stress.

"Let's go and ascend back up, out of here," he says. "I can help you ascend." We walk up, up, up, out of this terrible place, to my great relief. His strong arms hold me securely, and I am so glad that he came to rescue me. Mattheo then cleans and changes me and spends time rocking me until I have calmed down. This takes quite a while.

"This is why we ask you to do difficult and painful things at times; we are teaching you how to overcome your mortal flesh and its desires, so that you will not descend and remain forever in hell," he tells me. I am so traumatized, and so relieved that he rescued me, that I absorb and believe everything he is telling me without question. I have been rescued from hell by a father that loves me enough to go down into that terrible place after me, and I think that there can be no greater love. I love Mattheo at that moment with everything within me.

A female father, Joanna, one of the 12 fathers that I am bonded to and love deeply, then comes, and nurses me at the breast for a while, rocking me and singing to me softly. Hours later, I finally fall asleep. I decide to always, always do what the immortals say, and to never, ever give in to my mortal desires again.

This has been my introduction to "hell", one of the many horrible programming studios constructed by the Order to terrify their children into obedience. Many years later that I will learn that there are three stages located on three floors. Each level can be entered through winding stairs that go down into each level. Hell levels "one", "two" and "three" can be changed with a change of scenery, lighting, and children and/or adults dressed into costumes who either act as 'demons' or as 'tortured mortals', with appropriate props (including fake blood and gore), into hell levels "four", "five" and "six." The final and deepest level, utter darkness, reserved for the worst "sinners" who are completely "descended" is accomplished through time spent in an isolation tank or a negative sound room. There are usually about six or seven people being "tortured" at each level in this fake hell, but these rooms have mirrors that multiply the images until the scene appears to be filled with hundreds of writhing, tormented figures and flames, or screens that will playback such scenes.

But as an infant, and later as a toddler, I do not know these things. I fully believe that I have gone to hell. I have screaming nightmares at intervals about this place for years, until my systems learned to suppress them fully. But deep inside, I fear hell more than anything else. Every part inside of me fears this terrible place, the place where the worst possible punishments occur – or so I think, until there is a new, more terrible setup.

I am now a very young child, about age two years and two months. During the day, I disobeyed a direct command given to me by the father I love most, Mattheo. He has asked me to perform an act of sexual abuse on another child, and I can't. By this age, it is very, very rare that I say "no". Somehow, I identified too much with the child, who is close to my own age and who even looks like me, with curly brown hair and sad brown eyes. Mattheo is quietly angry, but he then goes on to abuse the child himself. Then, in order to punish me, he kills the child. I am heartbroken, but also feel glad that at least now, this child can no longer feel any pain or torment; she, at least, is set "free".

I later verbalize this feeling to Father Carlotti. "I know that she hurt, but now she will never hurt again," I say, using childish logic. "Nothing can hurt her anymore," I tell him. The fathers will view this a dangerous line of thinking, as rather than feeling remorseful and guilty about my disobedience, I am feeling that the child who died was "lucky". I am too young to realize that such thinking is unacceptable to the order, however.

In the middle of the night that follows this conversation, I am awakened by a "demon" who is older and larger than many that have visited me before. The "demon" takes me by the arm, yanking me roughly out of bed with claws that bite into my flesh until it bleeds. It hurries me down the black, winding staircase that descends into "hell". There are many adults and children tied to poles, and to my horror, right in front of me, in the center, is Father Mattheo. He is tied with rattling chains to a large pole of black stone. He is being lashed with a large flagellum, a whip that has bits of sharp rock and metal attached, and is screaming in pain.

"Satan" (another adult in costume) comes up to me and says, "You were supposed to take this punishment for disobedience, but Mattheo offered to take it instead. He is taking the punishment for your disobedience."

Horrified, I scream and weep as I see the blood pouring from Mattheo's wounds and the flagellum cuts deeper and deeper into him. I am terrified that he will die, this person who means so much to me, this person without whose love I don't believe I can survive.

"I'm sorry, I'm sorry," I scream.

Satan then turns to me, and says, "Do you vow to never disobey my mortal representative again?"

I stutter in my terror as I reply, "Y-y-yes."

Satan says, "Then take this spirit of obedience inside; it will punish you if you even think of disobeying." I do a short ritual, accept the spirit, bow low, and then "Satan" releases Mattheo from the pole with a golden knife. Mattheo is weak and shaky, but stumbles with me up the stairs, looking pale as we enter the room above.

He is taken to a healing room for healing technologies, and later comes and talks to me.

"I knew the punishment for your disobedience today would kill you, and I love you too much to lose you. I am older and stronger and offered to take it instead," he says. "You must learn that the actions of each of us affect those around us. The obedience or disobedience of one affects many others." He holds me as I cry for a long time, and then says, "I know you won't disobey me again; I know you love me too much."

This is the communal thinking of the Jesuit order. It is based upon loving one another and the terrible manipulation of attachment, and I am being indoctrinated into it in a very concrete way. I am learning that my rebellious thoughts, my saying "no", will cause pain to the people I love most, and it causes deep emotional pain. I am caught in a terrible place. I cannot choose what I truly want which is not obey commands to hurt others, because it will cause even more pain to the people I am attached to, and the child or person I try to save will just end up dying anyway. The cost of doing what I really want – to not hurt another child – could cause someone I love to be flogged to death. I fall asleep crying, wondering why the world is such as terrible place.

It is not until I am older, and learning to program other children, that I learn that the fathers take pain medication ahead of time during these setups and wear special rubber layers over their skin that releases 'blood' as they are being 'whipped'. Much of the screaming is acting, because the fathers are very, very good actors. As an older child, I am taught that these setups are a necessary thing to teach infants and young children about the real spiritual realities that they are too young to grasp yet. I accept this since I have already learned, even as a child, to never question my own programming.

When I remembered how the setups are done, and how the fathers I was bonded to manipulated me in this way, I was furious. I could not understand how one human being could do this to another. But then, I realized: they were afraid. If there is one thread that tied us all together, it was the deep, deep, terrifying fear that underlaid everything we did, the fear that sabotaged our real desire to love each other. We were all terribly, terribly afraid of these "immortals" who while appearing kind and loving, could also unleash terrible beings. The "immortals" are beings that the fathers believe control the universe and who oversee creation, and they worship them and give them unquestioning obedience. We were all slaves to our fear of these beings, and thus we could not act the way we truly wanted to. It would take finding a source of protection from this terror, much, much later in life, to break free of this slavery.

The Destruction of the Universe

I am two years old. The part of me who is out is a master controller named Galatea who is over the presentation systems. My hair has been dyed a beautiful silvery color, and I am wearing a black robe that has beautiful sparkly stars splashed over it. These little stars twinkle and glow as I walk. I love being the beautiful Galatea, one of the immortals who has been meeting with me since I was a tiny baby in my crib. I even speak with her soft, musical voice and inflection.

Pleiades is in the room with me. He is another master controller. Polaris, the third controller, sits on the other side. Satan, an adult in costume, is also there. He has more authority than even the master controllers in this setup.

In the room beneath the platform that the master controllers are sitting on, are other children my age dressed in costumes to represent various system controllers who will be working under me: Athena, Andromeda, and Saturn. Their sitting beneath the master controllers shows that they are lower in status – and thus obedient to – the master controllers who are sitting on an elevated platform. The children turn and look at me as Galatea, and at Satan.

Satan gives me the order. I must always, always immediately obey him, immediately and unfailingly.

"Take Andromeda, place her on her controller platform, and then have her give Athena the golden key. Athena will then leave the room, and in five minutes, will return with one of the presentation children".

I hurry to obey him. As a master controller, my obedience must be as quick as thought, or so I have been trained. I run to Andromeda, put her on her controller platform, and then tell Andromeda to give Athena the golden key and have her bring a child representing one of the presenters back into the room, going through a door marked with a special golden rune that means 'Wonderland'.

Andromeda stands, waiting. Athena goes to her, receives a golden key, and then goes through the door. We wait. And wait. Finally, she comes back through the special door with a child that resembles me. This child represents a presenter.

Satan then tells me, "Have Athena lock the child into her French shell." The shell is a clear plastic shell that will fit over the whole child. The child will be able to breathe due to special air holes.

The child is put into the shell, locked in, but then the trouble starts. The child starts screaming, saying that she wants out; that she doesn't want to be in the shell. Worse, she is not following her profile; the child is supposed to be speaking only French, but she is screaming in four different languages.

I hear a loud noise, and the child is knocked unconscious. But worse follows. The room that we, the immortal star systems are located in, turns black. The whole floor beneath us begins tilting, moving and spinning, as stars in the ceiling above begin falling, at times hitting me and the others in the room with sharp, biting pain. "The destruction of the universe has begun," Satan's voice thunders. "Andromeda, Athena, you both failed and allowed the presenter to fail, and now the universe will fall into chaos. You have become the bringers of chaos into the universe."

Pleiades, Polaris and others are screaming behind me. These are fathers I love, and I am causing them and everything and everyone I have ever loved to be destroyed, because of my failure. As a master controller, I must never, ever fail, and those who I oversee must never, ever fail, either. And I did. I failed to control the presenter.

I cower, screaming, as this terrible scene continues. I am overwhelmed with terror. Finally, Satan intervenes. "Do you swear that you will never allow failure in those beneath you?" he asks. "That as my representative to these mortals inside, that you will ensure that there will never be failure?" The shaking, tilting and spinning have slowed down while he talks, but the room is still dark.

I swear.

"Receive this spirit to help you," he then says. I look up, and a dark presence is standing next to him. I don't like it, but I don't want the universe to fail, so I nod "yes." It seems to melt into my body, and I feel terrible.

"I will give you another chance," Satan says. Instantly, the room completely stops shaking, tilting and spinning, and the lights come back on. I still feel shaken and disoriented by it all. I look, and Athena, played by my twin sister, also looks dazed and white-faced. The little girl in the shell is unconscious, and we have to pull her out after Athena unlocks the shell.

When the little girl comes back to consciousness, I tell her, "You must never, ever scream when you are put in the shell. It isn't forever; but if you scream or fight, worse happens than being in that shell."

The little girl nods her understanding. We redo the scene, and the little girl does not scream or fight this time. We all have just learned how very, very important it is to do our roles perfectly. The fate of the universe depends on it.

As the above memory shows, not only the master presentation controller Galatea, but also the sub-

controller Athena, and the presenter part beneath all of them, are all being taught the 'terrible consequences of disobedience' through the use of sophisticated programming studios that convincingly create terrible scenarios of devastation, disaster and pain. The Order uses many, many setups like these to instill complete obedience in all levels of a system. There will be other setups like this, until all of the controllers learn to do their jobs, including instantly punishing parts brutally for disobeying programming. These internal punishments that systems use to perpetuate programming long after the original programming sessions are usually memories, threats of, or internal reenactments of these terrifying traumas to keep parts in line. The capacity of parts to stop running such programs, i.e., stop obeying the original programming directives, can be greatly improved when parts realize that the 'disasters' were not natural consequences but staged trickery with no basis at all in any reality outside a programming studio, and that obedience only serves to benefit the cult without really protecting the child or his/her parts.

The Council of the Flesh and the Council of the Immortals

I am a year old, and a part inside that has been created through intense, agonizing pain has been called forward. This part, called "Mortal Flesh" is greeted by adults dressed in dark brown robes, the Council of the Flesh. "Flesh" is always associated with terrible pain, since it represents my mortal wants and desires, the things that keep me from ascending, according to the theology that I have been taught by the fathers.

The council head greets me, saying, "Welcome, mortal child. You are here to learn more about why it is important to overcome the flesh." I tremble a bit, because I do not like pain, but am able to cover my response and look expectantly at the figures.

"What are the primary sins of the flesh?" one of the council members asks me. I talked very early, as many of the infants in our facility do, in part due to genetic engineering for high IQs. I respond as taught: Unbelief, doubt, and disobedience – and forgetting eternity.

I have given the correct responses and they nod with satisfaction. Then Lovent, the council head, comes near me. This dark-clad figure takes my arm with one hand. In the other is a small candle. He speaks an incantation, and it lights with a flickering flame. He holds the candle flame to my arm for a period of time. I am in intense pain, sweating with the agony, but I do not pull away. Finally, with a deep burn on my arm, Lovent grunts his satisfaction with my desire to "overcome the flesh". If I had pulled away, or screamed,

I know that I would have been subjected to something even more painful. Terrible pain has been part of my life intermittently since I was in the womb, and my obedience to this council represents my deep-felt, instinctive desire to not experience even more pain.

I have been taught that the Council of the Flesh wants my best good and is teaching me to overcome my flesh so that I can ascend and join others who live in the celestial realms. Their greatest desire, they assure me, is to help me to avoid mortal hell, the fate for those who descend due to unbelief, doubt, and disobedience. By now, I have visited all seven levels of "hell" at the programming studio and agree heartily with them that this place is to be avoided at all costs. The Council of the Flesh has an eager, believing pupil for their theology.

I have already internalized this council, along with other councils such as the 12 members of the Mage Council, the Council of the Immortals, and the secret Vatican Council (which is not the public Vatican Council) inside. All leadership councils have 12 members, the number of governance, with it understood that Satan is the 13th member.

The Council of the Flesh by now has been internalized within me as well, and can cause intense pain in my body, and punish inside parts who seem to be following "fleshly desires" (e.g., not following their programming directives) instead of seeking immortality. If I seek eternity, and obey my programming, a member of the Council of the Immortals will call out one of my immortals inside and will take me up the golden stairway to the celestial realms as a reward.

At a year old, the celestial realms setup is more elaborate than when I was just a few weeks old. There are mists that glow everywhere, created by dry ice, and even a display of what looks like an aurora borealis above in the sky. The rich, fruity cream cake I am allowed to eat there makes me want to work hard to achieve permanent immortality, which I am assured I will be able to do one day.

I have a full operant conditioning system, reward and punishment, deeply installed by this age of one year old. The celestial realms are the "reward", and "hell" is the punishment system, for obedience and disobedience, respectively. If I disobey a command, I not only fear the anger of my programmer, I now fear descending for all of eternity into hell.

By this age, I have also internalized within my mind the hierarchy of councils that I have interacted with and been programmed by for the past year. These councils inside are the high controllers in my systems. They can mete out both punishment and reward internally, even in the absence of the external setups. This has been the real goal of these setups: to teach me to internalize the beliefs and behaviors and responses that the programmers have patiently been training me in over my time in the womb and the first year of my life. That is, they have made me a collaborator to and a perpetuator of my own abuse and control.

Chapter 3: Toddlerhood

My birth name is Lucient, but my daily name is Lucia. I am usually called Luce. This is the name of my 'cult host', or the part that presents during my cult life in the facility. As my cult life was the majority of my life until my escape in 2007, with only limited time in the presentations in different countries, Luce is the part of me who feels most like the 'real me'.

Mengele and Hilde work with me still, although my main influence are the fathers I love. Mengele and Hilde praise me for doing well and acting "intelligently" in different situations, but as Luce, I looked forward each day to the time I get to spend with the fathers I love.

For the first three years of life, life was regimented according to a strict routine. Early morning assessments are done quickly, with the fathers checking at regular intervals if prior programs installed are still intact. In between, there is holding and cuddling; these times too is scheduled. Later in the day, I learn the new day's task(s). There is always, always something new to be learned or practice designed to build further on old skills previously learned.

I felt like a miniature performer as the tasks continued day after day: learn to swim (and see how long I could endure in the water in one early test); learn to crawl across a narrow bridge with water on both sides, and see if I could push another baby crawling across the same bridge into the water; learn to open my little legs on cue from a trainer (for sexual training);

learn to switch out parts on cue with colored lights and tones, and many more tasks.

For the first three years, the children in the order are dressed in short white robes. Between three and five years old, the children wear brown tunics and leggings, then graduate to an acolyte's hooded brown robes at six years old. The older children find us younger children adorable. They enjoy interacting with me and the other infants, and will often come by and stroke our little cheeks and hands, or tell us that one day we will be big and have fun like they do. I love this attention and want to grow up to wear an acolyte's brown robe one day, and eventually at 13 years old, complete the coming of age ceremony and earn my adult name. I know that this will require learning many, many new skills and knowledge, and at this age, as the cult host, I am eager to learn.

Years later, when I was healing, I had trouble with the term "host", and especially its definition: an amnesic part that lives a life without abuse, or any knowledge of abuse. My host knew well that she was being raised within an occultic society. This was the only world she knew both as a child and as an adult. She knew about much of the abuse, and about the parts. She was allowed to watch and help monitor the different parts that presented when living in various countries. She was also one of my most deeply cult-loyal parts, because with all of her heart, she loved the fathers she had attached to. This feeling was true even during adulthood, which made leaving the order later in life very, very difficult. I missed the fathers when I didn't see or hear from them regularly, and not talking to them would trigger intense grief.

Control the Children

I am 12 months old. Father Jerome has tied me to his waist with a thick rope. He is playing the role of a system controller. My role is to obey everything he tells me, quickly and without error.

"Pick up those blocks," he says, "and stack the red ones together and the blue ones together." I quickly kneel by the blocks and do this task. When I am done, he says, "Good, good." In my role as a system part, I am learning how important instant obedience to my controllers is. The rope represents authority. The controller, being played today by Father Jerome, is always wearing the rope, and the system parts are tied to the controller by ropes.

It is a few days later. We are walking quickly and go to a field with lots of rocks. "Pick up the rocks, and put them in this corner of the field," he orders, pointing near the intersection of two stone walls. I begin picking up rocks while he oversees what I do. I am little and tire quickly, and his job is to encourage me to complete the task. Finally, we rest.

"You are listening well, and I am proud of you, Delta 34" he says. Jerome is dressed as Orgus, one of my delta controllers, and even in this menial task, I must obey him. The rocks represent memories, and he is teaching me to take them and put them in the correct area of the field. The field is divided up into squares labeled with various names and runes. I must match the rock and its rune with the storage rune.

After a period of rest, we eat some bread and drink some water then go back to our task. "Delta 34, put these memories into this storage file," Orgus commands, pointing to an area of the field marked with a rune that means "Low security". Quickly, obediently, I do so. "Delta 34, pass this memory into this file," he commands again, and I take the rock into a storage file marked "Medium security." I already know that rocks that are "high security" must be passed back to Orgus, to put into a special high security vault deep beneath us.

I am 18 months old. I have a rope tied around my waist. I am a gamma system controller, and tied to me by thick ropes are small children of my own age. There are six children. I have been told that my job is to ensure that they are completely obedient to me. These children represent my system parts. My job is to protect them by ensuring obedience to all commands from the programmers.

"You can walk around this house, but do not touch any of the candy in the yellow room," I am told by Father Carlotti, who is dressed in the costume of a master controller from the galaxy Pleiades. He has the stars of Pleiades scattered over a dark, midnight blue sky, and is wearing the runes and codes that signify his status. System controllers such as gamma system controllers take their orders from master controllers inside. Their orders must always, always, be utterly obeyed.

The children and I walk together into different rooms in the house. I have to tug on the ropes of a few to get them to follow. One room is painted with bright yellow walls, and this color, and the huge table in the middle of the room, attract us all. The children and I eagerly walk towards the table, where there are piles of candies in glass bowls.

The children are hungry, since they have not eaten yet, and it is midday. They begin pulling me towards the table. "No, no, children!" I say desperately. "We were told not to touch the candy."

I try to pull them away, but I am not strong enough to stop all of them pulling at me at once. One little girl, who looks so much like me, grabs a piece of soft divinity off the table and starts eating it. I try to pull her away, but it is too late; she has disobeyed the order.

Suddenly, she jerks in a violent seizure, turning blue. The other children stop their own rush towards the table. With frightened eyes we watch as this child continues seizing, and then dies. The candy must have poison in it, and she has disobeyed and died as a result. But I am responsible for her obedience, and with guilt and shame, realize that it is my fault that she died.

Pleiades (Father Carlotti) comes into the room and looks with anger and disgust at what has happened. "You killed her!" he tells me. "You didn't make sure she obeyed you! A controller always makes sure that their system obeys them. You failed her!"

I feel terrible, but worse is to come. Now, as I move with the children around the house, I must drag this dead child around with me.

"You are feeling the weight of your failure," Pleiades (Father Carlotti) says. I feel terrible, and start crying. A child, one put into my care, has died, because I failed to ensure her obedience to a command from the master controller for my system. I crumple to the floor, heartbroken, as I weep.

"Stop crying and do your job," he says sternly. "Don't let any more of your children die."

He then gives another command. "Do not let any of the children touch the toys in the blue room." The blue room is one we saw when walking through, but on this round of the house, I see toys on the floor: blocks of various colors, puzzles, picture books, and sparkly, beautiful dolls and balls. The children, who seem intent on disobeying me in spite of what happened in the yellow room, try to pull me over with them to the toys on the floor.

"No, no, children, no!" I scream. I pull with all of my strength, trying to pull them away. But the children wear me down, and one of them picks up a shiny red ball. Suddenly, there is a scream, and the child falls down dead. With a feeling of despair, I realize that this toy, too, contains poison. I am now dragging two dead children around from the ropes tied to my waist, and I am very tired. But the other children are now very quiet and seem willing to listen to me when I tell them not to touch anything at all in the house unless I give them permission. We sit in the middle of a red room, and Pleiades (Father Carlotti) enters. "You may all have a drink of juice," he says, and he pours out a cup for each of us. The juice tastes good, and I am relieved that no death results.

"Only allow them to do the things I tell you to," he says. "This is the only way to ensure their safety." I nod my understanding.

The children and I stay in this terrible house for two days. I am dragging the two dead children, reminders of what happens when system controller allows parts to disobey their master controller. During the day, Pleiades (Father Carlotti) comes at intervals, and lets us eat, or allows us to play with only certain toys, or rest. The children, who are still alive, and I sleep together, utterly exhausted by the end of the day, tied together, on a mat on the floor.

By the second day, the bodies of the two children who died begin to smell. The other children and I feel ill from the smell, and Pleiades (Father Carlotti) returns. "You are smelling the stench of disobedience," he tells us. I wonder how long I must drag these bodies around. I am feeling tired, ill, and sick of it all.

Finally, Pleiades returns again, gives a code, and I go inside. He then unties me from the children, and Lucia, my cult host, is sent out to take a shower and then rest in my dorm room. I am tired indeed and realize that being a controller is a great responsibility. The lives of those under me depend upon my ensuring complete obedience. I go to sleep, dreaming of saving children, while I am yelling orders at them, frantic to save their lives.

This memory caused me to cry for days when I first had it. I felt overwhelmed by guilt, sadness, grief, and then, finally, anger at Carlotti and the other fathers for putting me through such a terrible setup at such a young age. This is how the Jesuits train the internal controllers and master controllers to do their jobs: it is at the threat of loss of life if they should fail, not just for them, but for those they are supposed to protect.

I now realized why for years, my system controllers had been fighting me so hard, when I asked them to stop doing their cult jobs. They were desperately, desperately, trying to save the lives of children that they loved. They were terrified to disobey the master controllers over them inside, who I had yet to meet at that point in my healing. The lessons of absolute obedience, of never failing, and of controlling inside parts, had been instilled through this and numerous similar setups.

The Cages

I am two years old. I am sitting in a small metal cage that is just big enough for me to curl up in. I am in a cage on the bottom row of a small pyramid comprised of four levels of cages, stacked one on top of each other. The bottom row has six cages, the next row above has four cages, then two cages in the next row above, and finally one cage at the very top. Each cage contains a child. We are all close in age.

I feel liquid dripping down on me. Someone in one of the cages above me has urinated on me. I hate the sticky, smelly urine. But my hair is matted with worse: the soft liquid stool that another stressed child in one of the upper cages has evacuated. I feel filthy, frightened, and the smell is horrible. I can see Mengele and Hilde, his assistant, in another part of the room.

I am hungry and thirsty. It has been a whole day since I have had anything to eat or drink. I whimper, and a guard comes by, looks into my cage, and drags me out. He rapes me roughly, and then puts me back into the cage. I feel utterly humiliated and utterly defiled.

Mengele walks towards the cages and opens the door to mine. He draws me out of the cage, and then takes me into another room where Hilde is waiting. He places me onto a mark chalked on the floor; it is a small blue square.

"Stand in the square," he orders me. I do so.

In front of me is a large red circle painted on the floor, and in the middle of the circle is a small infant. Mengele places a knife in my hand, and then gives a single command: "Kill!" I hesitate for a second, struggling with killing this tiny, defenseless baby with red, wrinkled face and fisted up, tiny hands. I have practiced before with kittens, strangling them with my bare hands at his order, but this is different.

Finally, I stab the infant. But I had hesitated. Mengele is displeased with me. "You must never hesitate!" he yells at me. Delayed obedience will not work with him. I am put back in the same cage, and am told by Hilde, "No food or water until you don't hesitate". I am trembling with hunger and thirst. The terrible smell in my cage and on my body makes me retch. I wonder if I will die here.

Eight hours later, Hilde comes and takes me out of the cage. I am being given a second chance to be obedient. Once again, I am placed on the blue square. Once again, there is a tiny baby inside the red circle. Mengele is there. I am weaving a bit from trauma and exhaustion, but I listen carefully. The order comes abruptly again: "Kill!" and this time, without hesitation, I obey.

"Good girl, I knew you would learn," Mengele praises me. Hilde smiles, and gives me a drink of water, and some soft pudding. "Not too fast, eat slowly," she warns, since I have not eaten in almost two days.

Hilde then takes out a sponge, and with warm water that feels wonderful, washes the feces out of my hair. She then sponges the filth off of my naked body. "Good girls get to smell good," she murmurs to me in German. "No one wants to smell bad, like a bad girl." I am grateful for the food and bath, and already feel a little better. Maybe I won't die. But I am also feeling sad deep inside about the little baby that has just died. But I know, oh how I know, that I cannot show any of this sadness to these two. I lock the tears deep, deep inside, handing the emotion over to parts whose job is to contain the sadness and grief.

Mengele and Hilde then take my hand, and together, they put me into one of the cages on the second tier. I have performed well, and so now only three cages are above mine. This tier gets a little bit of water and a slice of bread twice a day, and there are fewer feces and showers of urine to endure. Best of all, I am only raped once a day, instead of four times a day as I was on the lowest tier.

After this, each day, twice a day, I am taken into the room with the blue square and the red circle with a baby in the middle, and I am given the order to "Kill!" I perform well. I have seen children on the bottom row weaken and lay in their cages without moving, and I wonder how many times they have hesitated. Some end up dying, and their bodies remain there for several days as a warning to those who fail to obey instantly.

On the fourth day, instead of a baby, it is a toddler tied up in the middle of the red circle. The child is struggling and screaming, and when the order "Kill!" comes, I hesitate.

Mengele looks furious. Without a word, Hilde takes me back to the cages. I am back in one of the bottom ones, starting out all over again. The rapes every six hours start back up, and I am covered with urine and feces at the end of the next day, hungry and thirsty once more.

I know that if I stay here, I will die. The smell of the decomposing body in the cage next to mine is an object lesson in what happens to children who are on the bottom row too long.

After 24 hours, Hilde comes and gets me, and takes me back into the room with the blue square and red circle. Once again, a struggling toddler is tied up in the middle of the circle. Mengele gives the order again, and this time, I obey his command instantly, without hesitation.

"Good girl, you have learned," he croons. "My little killer is learning." Hilde again bathes me, feeds me, and once again, I am moved back to the second tier of cages. I never hesitate again. Over and over, I am given the command to kill, twice a day, and soon my response is automatic; I obey without conscious thought.

After another few days, I am in the cage at the top. I am now killing on command using various weapons – knife, a needle, a garrote. Finally, I am praised heavily, and allowed to leave the cages, the terrible cages. I was 25 months old and have learned to disconnect how much I hated taking a life from conscious thought.

Mengele's methods of programming children were cruel beyond belief. But the occultic societies recognized that he got results: a child who survived his methods would be completely programmed and obedient. This is why he was so sought after by various occultic groups around the world. For a large fee, he would go in and train children of all ages, using his primitive but effective methods which were based on data collected for years.

Sadly, he was a head trainer for the Jesuits in their main training facility and labs. He used these labs to continue his experimentation on humans, which meant that the infants and children who lived in this facility would be exposed to his merciless training. I was extremely relieved when he died when I was 19 years old, and another, younger head trainer who used better methods that did not cause such needless loss of life (or sanity, in some children) took charge of the training and experiments. The younger head trainer was my mentor, and when I became older, I replaced her as head of this facility. But I consulted with her frequently, because I admired her more humane approach and her deep insights into human behavior. She was one of my best friends, and I loved her deeply.

Alice in Wonderland

In Jesuit programming, when presenters are not 'out' in the body, they are living in 'Wonderland' inside. In the Order, Alice in Wonderland programming is used to ensure that presenters: never communicate with or be aware of other parts inside; completely believe that their memories of an ordinary life is the only life that that person is living; stay completely amnesic to any cult activity; and stay completely unaware of any loss of time when they are not 'out' in the body. Key characters in Wonderland, such as the White Rabbit, remind presenters of these tasks, and reward and punish for compliance or disobedience as needed. As these memories relate, Alice in Wonderland programming begins at a very early age.

I am 18 months old. I am in a special place in the outdoor programming lab. It is a sunny, warm day, and the sun falls on my face and shoulders as I walk on slightly chubby but muscular legs into an opening within a boxwood maze. This opening is a beautiful arched trellis covered with roses and other climbing flowers, with sweet perfume filling the springtime air.

There is a path that I can see that leads through this maze, which is augmented in various places with trees, shrubs, and even a fake "seashore" on the shores of a small lake. I wait, enjoying the weather, which is sunny and bright. Soon, an older child dressed as Alice from Wonderland appears. She is about 11 years old, has beautiful curly, dark blond hair and light blue eyes. She is dressed in a blue dress covered with a white pinafore, and she has a big blue bow in her hair that matches her pretty eyes perfectly.

The girl guides me by the hand along the path. An adult, Mattheo, my primary trainer, is dressed like a large white rabbit, and I toddle along behind him, being guided by "Alice". I am a French presenter named

"Jean". This will be my name when I spend time in France with my French family, starting at age three. As 'Jean', I have had careful programming since birth to come out and go back in on cue, and to understand French when it is spoken to me. It is the only language that I, as Jean, have ever heard in this presentation.

As Alice guides me, she warns me, "Never, ever leave the path. If you do, terrible, terrible things will happen. The only safety is to follow the white rabbit, and to stay on the path. Never leave it, regardless of what happens." I wonder what could happen that is so terrible but prefer not to find out. I have already experienced "terrible, terrible" already numerous times in my young life, and have no desire to experience it again.

The white rabbit leads us to a special area with a small stone bench, and pretty stone pavers cover the ground in the center. This area is in a large room-like area in the maze surrounded by boxwood "walls" to nearly enclose it. At the entrance that we pass through is a sign overhead written in golden runes that signify "France". I follow the white rabbit and Alice inside.

"Jean, this is where you will live in Wonderland," both Alice and the white rabbit tell me in unison. "This is your special place," the white rabbit repeats. I have heard these same instructions before, on previous visits.

On the walls of the boxwoods, which are high – nearly seven feet in height – are large television screens that display pictures of my family in France playing with me as a baby, talking to me in French. The screens show me the cottage that I will live in when I go to France for the first time in another year and a half. On the video display, I hear my French mother, Jeanine, talking to me as a baby in loving tones, as she changes me. I see her take me outside to see the flowers in the cottage garden outside the house. These are the 'memories' of 'France' that Jean is supposed to have.

Alice cautions me, "You must never, ever leave this area when you are not called outside to present," she tells me sternly.

The white rabbit looks at me and repeats her warning. "You must not leave, even to go to other parts of Wonderland, ever," he insists.

I have heard this warning before, since this is not my first visit to the French part of Wonderland. The first few times, Alice and the white rabbit stayed with me and played, speaking French to me. There are toys, games, and other things to play with, even picture books with words in French on the cover. And the fascinating, fascinating videos of a wonderful life with a loving family in France play constantly. I will not be bored here.

"You must remain here when you are told to," Alice says again, and then she and the white rabbit leave. This is the first time I have been left here, and I wonder how long I will be alone.

In a little while, I hear a little girl singing and laughing outside the entrance to my special place. I look out, and see that she is about three years old, and has curly brown hair and merry green eyes. The little girl stops at the entrance to French wonderland, peeks her head in, and in English says, "Little girl, come out and play with me."

She seems to be very nice, her smile is welcoming, and I am getting tired of playing alone. The sun is shining, and she beckons with her hand outstretched to me. I walk over to her and take her hand, and we walk together down the path.

But suddenly, a large, dark bird-like creature swoops overhead. "The Jabberwocky!" the little girl screams, letting go of my hand and diving under a bush. I try to do the same, but rough hands grab me and pinch me, and two fat people take me to a corner, and rape me. The hands belong to two men dressed in striped costumes, and I learn that they are "Tweedle Dee" and "Tweedle Dum" and that they enjoy hurting little presenters who leave the place they are supposed to stay in.

I begin crying and try to make my way back to the French part of Wonderland. I hear a cacophony of voices babbling in various languages as I pass by entrances to other parts of the maze. Finally, completely lost, I go into an enclosed part of the maze where the people speak German. There is a little girl who looks like me, having lunch with her family at a round wooden table in the center of the enclosed area. "Help me!" I wail in French.

"A foreigner, a foreigner!" The family jumps to their feet, shouting in rage. Then they all rise up and stab me with their sharp forks and knives, and hurt me, including hurting me in my privates. I am screaming in terror at this point, as the German speakers say "We hate French speakers who come into our area. Stay out, you are NOT welcome here!" Traumatized and shaking, I am thrown out of this part of Wonderland, and lay on the ground, terrified. Suddenly, the white rabbit and Alice are bending over me.

"Why didn't you stay in your area, where you would be safe?" Alice asks sorrowfully.

"We tried to spare you this type of pain, but you didn't believe us," says the white rabbit with heartbreak in his eyes.

Slowly, they lead me back to the French area of Wonderland, where the French videos are playing. I try to explain about the little girl who tricked me into leaving.

"You will see and hear a lot of people and things that might seem to be fun, or that might make you want to leave your area," cautions Alice. "But you must never, ever listen to them. Only leave when the white rabbit tells you to; and only go where he tells you to. He will make sure that you stay safe."

The white rabbit looks at me tenderly, and I realize that he really does want to protect me from the terrible things that happen outside of the French part of wonderland.

"Why were the German people so mean to me?" I sob. "I haven't done anything to make them hate me!"

"They hate you because you left your area and are breaking the rules. If you break them, everyone, including them, are put into danger," explains the white rabbit. "You put them in extreme danger when you were talking to them; they might all have been killed."

I am horrified at the thought. I am a French presenter, and so am completely amnesic to the rituals and sacrifices that I have attended, including the ones I have done to seal me into my own presentation and create barriers between me and other presentations. The hedges in Wonderland are a physical representation of these barriers, which I had crossed in my terror a few minutes before.

"Never, ever cross into another area," says Alice. "You have experienced what can happen if you do."

I certainly have. Alice and the White Rabbit leave again, and this time, in spite of hearing children skipping and singing outside my boxwood enclosure, calling out to me in various languages, inviting me to play with them, I refuse to leave, and obediently stay in my area. I am learning to ignore the other presentations in this very concrete way, and to stay inside, immune to the attractions of other lives and other languages, staying exactly where I am told internally. As I get older and start training to be a programmer myself, only then do I learn that the 'Jabberwocky' is a flying animatronic or a drone controlled by the programmers.

The setup described above is used to teach parts to never cross the perimeters and barriers between the different presentations, thus isolating parts from each other. This isolation makes the person more controllable as each part will only have a partial view of the person's lived reality. Most importantly, it terrifies the presenters into obeying the rules to never communicate with each other and to never pay attention to anything outside their designated internal zones. Otherwise, because children have natural curiosity, the different presenters might be tempted talk to each other, or to "peek out" when the other parts are presenting in their respective countries. This kind of internal communication or shared presenting would overcome the amnesia or barriers between presentations, which is considered critical to maintaining security and covers. Many exposures to these setups and special rituals are used to make the child internalize the mazes and Wonderland, and to keep presenters in their designated zones when they are not cued out.

When not out presenting, the parts will be trained to watch the videos within their special area, augmented with videos of actual events, and to accept these videos as their own 'memories'. This creates the perception of a sustained and unbroken timeline for the presenters who will believe that they are continuously "living life". They are thus not able to perceive that they are 'inside' and have in fact 'lost time' from the time intervals (which can be significant, lasting months) between being called out to present. For instance, if a child has not been sent to a presentation for many months, they will be shown videos of significant events that the child allegedly experienced during this time. Thus, Jean will have her own "memories" of childhood, with many important events "remembered", in spite of the fact that in reality, she only spends three weeks a year in France, trading *out with her twin sister and other children who look like her in this role. All have been equally programmed to look, act, and sound like "Jean", and the families are also programmed to not notice when 'Jean' is played by different children at different times. The Order will typically conceive several children (two to four is an average number) that look alike, making such 'swapping' possible when necessary.*

I am two and a half years old. I am outside a special room in the programming lab, dressed in a bright blue dress that falls just beneath my knees, and a white pinafore. My hair has been dyed yellow with a temporary dye. I have a large white bow in my hair, along with white stockings and shiny shoes. I am Alice, one of the main presentation controllers, and I am going to a tea party. I love tea parties, with cakes and tea to eat and drink, and I look forward to this. Next to me, holding my hand, is Mnemosyn. In my Alice in Wonderland programming, she is a mother figure to me, Alice. Mnemosyn takes me places, reminding me of what to remember and what to forget. Mnemosyn also helps me to "remember to forget". I look at her and smile, and she smiles back.

We enter the room and sit at the tea party table. Several fathers I love are sitting at the table. But there is something wrong, terribly wrong. As I look at them, to my horror, I realize that these beloved fathers have been killed in terrible, gruesome ways: one father has his eyes gouged out, and is slumped blankly on his chair, unseeing with dark, bloody holes in his face. Another father has blood pouring out of his mouth, as he sits in pale, bloody death. The one next to him has his arms amputated. Blood has been pouring out in spurts and covers his robes. Across from him, a father has her chest stabbed and her breasts cut off. Her mutilated body leans at a grotesque angle in her chair. Each of the twelve chairs holds a gruesome, terrible scene of a recent death of a father I love.

I start screaming in horror.

"What are you screaming about?" Mnemosyn asks calmly, as she sits and pours tea for me out of a large teapot. "You seem upset about something."

I cannot believe what she is saying. It is obvious what I am upset about! "The fathers!" I cry out in anguish. "They're dead! Someone has killed them!"

Mnemosyn stops, looks at me, and says, "Alice, there are no dead fathers here. It's just you and I. Now stop being silly, and let's enjoy our tea". She points to an empty chair for me to sit in, and fills my cup with tea, passing me a plate with biscuits on it. "Have one, they're especially good," she says, completely ignoring the gruesome scene around us.

I feel green, but have learned to always obey Mnemosyn, whose job is to tell me what to believe and what not to believe – or remember. As she calmly munches on a biscuit and sips tea, she tries to discuss the outing that we will have in a bit to the beach. But I am white-faced and have difficulty not looking at the gruesome scene around the table.

"You look upset," she says in a slightly critical tone.

"But, the fathers," I say again, pointing to one of the dead fathers who has been murdered next to me to illustrate my point.

"Alice, you must stop imagining such things," she scolds. "If I say they aren't here, they aren't here. Why can't you listen to me? Don't you think I would be upset if there was something here to see?" As she continues to lecture me, I finally calm down and have a sip of tea with sugar from the beautifully decorated teapot: it has lovely roses and flowers on it, and golden runes in a lovely design.

"Good, Alice, you are looking better," Mnemosyn praises me. "You really shouldn't go around talking about dead bodies that aren't there. That's what gets people locked up in the insane asylum. Listen to me, and that will never happen to you."

She is reassuring in her tone. Then, she says, "Do you agree to believe everything – and I mean everything

– that I tell you, and to ignore completely the things I tell you to?" Her eyes look fierce as she says this, and I say "Yes" in a low voice.

She then takes me to a small altar in one corner of the room, and we do a sacrifice together; I put a small child on the altar and stab it through the eyes, as I say "I will only see what you, Mnemosyn, tell me to see," and then stab it in the head, saying "I will only remember what you, Mnemosyn, tell me to remember." She pats me on the head, praising me, as I invoke a demonic spirit of memory control to come inside and help me to always listen to Mnemosyn. Afterwards, we turn around, and I am startled. The table has been completely cleaned up; there are no gruesome bodies, and the tablecloth is sparkling white. The tea party looks just as it should, with colorful flowers in a vase. I join Mnemosyn at the table who with a smile says, "See, Alice? There were no bodies here. You were just having a bad dream. Always, always bring your bad dreams to me, and I will help them go away."

I feel rather dazed. Deep inside, I wonder if the fathers I love are okay, dream or no dream. It was all too real, what I saw before the sacrifice. But Mnemosyn carries on a bright, happy conversation. I finish having tea with her and the other characters from Wonderland who have come to join us: Dormouse, the Mad Hatter, the White Rabbit. These are all children or fathers I love, dressed in costumes, but they play their parts perfectly, and we have a good time.

Later, I tremble just slightly as I leave the programming lab to return to my room. On the way, I see Mattheo and Jerome together; they smile at me and look just fine; they act as if nothing at all has happened in that terrible room; they certainly aren't dead, or even hurt. I wonder, then, if it really was all just a bad dream as Mnemosyn insisted.

This "tea party" setup was an essential part of developing my presenter amnesia controllers, Alice and Mnemosyn. In these setups, Mnemosyn, the adult programmer and a mother figure to young Alice, is modeling to her the behaviors and beliefs expected of the non-cult presentations if they ever remember any cult-related memories, and shows her how to handle them with denial and amnesia. The two of them work together to take memories of violent cult rituals or other events that a presenter might have, and to consign these memories into the categories of "bad dreams" which are not to be believed. That is, they are dedicated to ensuring presenter amnesia and denial of cult life. This enables the presenters to keep believing that their 'ordinary lives' are the only life they have ever lived, and that they have never experienced ritual abuse or mind control.

By the time I am five, Alice is able to check if any non-cult presenter is experiencing any unauthorized or 'bleed through' memories of their cult life, cult events, or lives of other presenters. If this is happening, she can help the presenter to completely forget them with the help of the ever-watchful and careful Mnemosyn. Of course, my cult host is allowed to remember cult life so Alice does not interact with her. If Lucia, my cult host, has any memories that need to be forgotten, these will be stored within a completely different high-security storage system that has different guardians and barriers.

Because Alice, Mnemosyn, and the other Wonderland parts have critical controller roles, they undergo frequent reinforcement of their programming through not only physical setups but the use of virtual reality and other technologies. As usual, the setups are designed to create complete amnesia, and to teach Alice to help the presenters to only remember what they are told to remember. These setups are at times brutally violent in order to make the threat of what could happen, if a presenter remembers things that they shouldn't, seem absolutely believable.

Over the next few months, the presenters themselves will be hosted in the various countries they are to live in at times. Before doing so, they will experience numerous physical setups in which the lives of their (beloved) family members – father, mother, sister, brother, aunt, grandmother, etc. – in various countries will be threatened should they ever remember their cult experiences, or the memories of parts that present in other countries. Finally, before starting to live with the family for a few weeks in France, or Germany, or another country, a "baby" brother in each of these families is killed by the young child who is to live and present in these countries. This creates extra guilt (along with terror created by the threat of the family "telling" and the child being sent to "prison") which will help to maintain the complete amnesia required.

Shell Programming

I am a presentation controller named Andromeda. I am two and a half years old. My job is to make sure that the presentation shells are working correctly, and that only the parts in the presenting shell are allowed to see, hear or speak. Other presentation parts, while not out in their respective shells, are not allowed to see, speak or hear. My instructions are clear: ONLY the child locked into the shell (with a special key) is allowed to see, hear or speak. The others must be silent, and unaware of what the child in the shell says or does.

Today, I am practicing controlling the French shell and the French parts who present through this shell. My twin sister, Lizzie, is playing the role of the French presenter today. She is wearing the clear flexible plastic shell that represents the shell program. My twin sister Lizzie, as Jean (we both play this presentation role in France, so she plays her role perfectly) is speaking in French to her French mother, who is in the programming studio to assist with this program. To help teach the other presentation parts who are not currently out in their respective shells that they must not see, hear or speak, children labeled with runes that represent other presentations are standing behind me. They are wearing eye patches, ear plugs, and blindfolds over their mouths to prevent their seeing, hearing, or speaking anything

While Lizzie is talking, I am doing my other, critical job: as a presentation controller, I am monitoring Jean to ensure that her language, her apparent intellect, her body language, and her motor skills are perfectly in line with her presentation profile designed by the programmers. If she deviates even slightly, or tries to take her shell off, she will be tortured terribly, and so will I. If I fail to report even the slightest deviation to

Pleiades, Polaris, or Galatea, my own controllers and the triad of master controllers over all of the presentation systems, they and I will be tortured terribly. Father Mattheo, the person I love most, is Pleiades, and I am desperate that I perform well and not fail. I don't want him tortured. The three master controllers are sitting quietly on an elevated platform above the scene, which represents their more ascended status: the higher the controller, the higher in the room they sit. These master controllers are dressed in robes covered with stars representing their galaxy, watching, just as they will do internally as I grow and the program is fully installed.

Jean performs perfectly, even not understanding English when one of her mother's friends comes by, looks at Jean, and asks her a question in English. Since in her French presentation, Jean does not understand English, she gives the woman a smile, and a look of bewilderment. Jean has passed her test, and I am relieved.

Pleiades approaches me where I am standing on my little, raised platform above the children representing various presenters. He gives a verbal code, flashes a special pattern on the handheld device that he shows me, and also shows me his golden key. I must see all of these things, along with his voice and face, in order to obey his command to change shells. This has been practiced thousands of times over the past two years. I obey instantly. He has given me the code to change shells, replacing the French shell out in front with the Russian shell. I have a lever that rotates the correct shell out to the place in the room that represents the shell being out in the body. I relay the command to Athena, my sub-controller, who goes and gets another little girl. This little girl represents Katerina, or Katya as she is called by friends and family, and she is my Russian presenter. I must make sure that the shell is in place perfectly, locked in so that the little girl cannot remove it, and then monitor her performance as Katya. I give the key to Athena, the controller under me, who locks the shell with the little girl in it into place, and returns the key to me.

Katya's sister in the family that she will live with when she is in Russia, who is also a Jesuit child, comes into the room, and starts speaking Russian. Katya is performing well: her body language, language skills and abilities seem consistent with her profile. Then, an older man with white hair comes into the room. He is holding another little girl by the hand. The little girl comes over to Katya, and asks her in German, "What is your name?" as she smiles.

Katya answers, "Katya." I am horrified. She has broken with her presentation profile, disobeying her programming to only know Russian. I hear a sharp "zap!" and Katya falls over unconscious. I hear another zap, and I am shocked throughout my body with terrible, excruciating pain.

Pleiades and the other master controllers come over. They are angry. "She failed, and that means you failed!" they tell me. "Your life, and the lives of your presenters, depend upon never, ever breaking profile. Things like this can never, ever be allowed to happen!"

I am heartbroken. I failed, and Katya almost died. I am responsible for her, and her failure means that I had failed her.

The next day I am given another chance. Another little girl, one of my sisters who is presenting as Katya, plays her part perfectly. I have been given a new tool: a wand that can instantly stun a presenter into unconsciousness if they falter or deviate slightly from their profile. This way, they won't have to get hurt and possibly die, as I am told could happen if they continue to fail.

"You can prevent their deaths, if you discipline them swiftly and correctly," Polaris tells me. "Punishing them for disobeying – even slightly – will save their lives, and mine."

I feel the weight of this responsibility. Being a high-level controller over presentations is a very difficult job.

But I desperately, desperately want to save the lives of the people I love, and my own life, so I will learn to do this job, and do it well.

As time goes on, there are fewer and fewer infractions or variances from the presentation profiles, under my watchful eye. These are punished immediately and painfully, and as I have been taught to do, I report the deviations to the three master controllers over me. They will notify Saturn, my presentation reprogramming system, and tell him which internal reprogramming sequences to run that night to fix the errors and repair the system. The fathers want our systems to be able to self-reprogram, because we may be in situations where we are away from Rome, and unable to get to a programming facility for a period of time.

As this memory shows, the presentation programming that I underwent was quite complex, where my internal controllers and master controllers were taught to do their jobs by the programmers using concrete setups to model the expected behaviors and train these controllers. The punishments for any infractions are very severe in order to instill the importance of never breaking presentation when being hosted in another country outside of the facility. Internally, Athena, the part who works under Andromeda, goes to the entrance portal of Wonderland and tells the white rabbit to bring the correct presenter. Pleiades informs Andromeda which presenter this is, and Andromeda will pass this command on to Athena. The white rabbit and Alice together will bring the correct presenter to Athena, who will then go to Andromeda, get the key to lock the presenter into her shell, and then return the key to Andromeda.

When the child's designated time in the presentation is over for the time being, Andromeda will give Athena the key to unlock the presenter from the shell. She then returns the presenter to the rabbit hole where Alice will be waiting for the presenter. Alice then takes the presenter by the hand and leads her down the rabbit hole and back into Wonderland, taking her back to the correct area within it. At this point, depending on the orders given by Pleiades, Andromeda will have another presenter brought out, to be locked into the appropriate shell, or other controllers may have the cult host or other cult parts present, according to what the cult needs at that point.

The concern about breaking presentation is a concern that if a child acts "differently" and their profiles are not "perfect", then the cover story that the little girl has only lived in America, or that she grew up in France and has never traveled elsewhere, could be *questioned. If a child looks "multiple", or "abused", this could also draw undue attention and scrutiny from others, which is the last thing that the Jesuits want. For the children are used to help conceal the criminal activities worldwide that the Order is involved in, once they are hosted in various nations.*

Chapter 4: Theta and Spiritual Systems Training

Some of the events described in this chapter on theta and spiritual training may stretch the limits of believability. Based on my memories, in order to train their children in these skills and indoctrinate them in their occult teachings, the Order uses real spiritual experiences as well as elaborate setups with costumes and props, virtual reality and other technologies, drugs and hypnosis. Both types of experiences will feel very real to the child who is going through it. It can be difficult to distinguish whether a memory is of a real spiritual experience, or of a contrived scenario carefully staged by the adults. In this chapter, I describe the events as I experienced them as a child, when they felt completely real to me. While I personally believe that the events I have chosen to describe in this chapter were indeed authentic spiritual experiences, I am also open to the possibility that they were staged and based upon trickery.

Theta Training

The room is dark with absolutely no light in it. I am only three months old, in a crib. I am gumming on a toy that I have been given to play with: a severed human head.

With my tiny fingers, I explore its matted hair, its eyes, its mouth. I am a theta controller named Nemesis in training. Darkness has been the main realm that I live in. I only feel comfortable in this dark. This and similar body parts have been my playthings.

Later, Father Carlotti comes into the room. He places steel blades on the ends of my little feet, and tells me to kick hard. I kick as hard as I can. They encounter the soft fur of a rabbit that squeals. My kicks have killed it. Carlotti lifts me up, hugs me, and praises me. "This is where your power comes from," he tells me in a soft voice. "You really are a little killer." I feel funny about his praise. I am glad that he is happy, but deep inside, I don't like being called a "killer".

A few months later, Father Jerome comes into the room to take me for my daily training. I am not feeling good, in fact, I feel ill, and do not want to go. So, I think about hitting Jerome in the head with a tiny fist, even though he is too far away to reach, to let him know where I hurt. I simply think it. Father Jerome steps back, looking surprised, and then goes to get Father Carlotti. "She hit me with theta skill," he tells Carlotti. Carlotti is surprised and objects, "That's impossible. She's much too young."

Jerome lifts me up and praises me for what I have done. He checks my head and gives me some medicine to help with the headache and slight fever. "You were trying to tell me what was wrong, weren't you?" he says in a loving voice. I had and am glad that he figured it out. But I am also pondering the fact that I can think something, will it, and others feel it. It seems like a wonderful new thing to be able to do.

I am nine months old and have been taught by Father Mattheo to direct my theta blows at animals. I can now kill an animal easily with a quick blow. For some reason, he and the other fathers seem excited by this ability. I hate the terrible scream the animals make as I kill them, but they tell me that what I am doing is good, very, very good indeed.

I wonder why an activity that makes me so sad makes them so happy. It makes me feel strange and dirty inside. I hate the rituals that have to be done before and after the kills to "give power". I hate the killing. But I cannot let them know this. They will be angry, and I might even have to visit "hell". I don't want that.

Today is a bit different. Mattheo brings a small child that I have never seen before into the room and tells me to hit the child hard with my theta ability. I don't want to do this and look upset. Mattheo sits me on his lap and talks to me. "Nemesis, this is a very, very bad child that has hurt a lot of other children in terrible ways. If this child is allowed to grow up, he will become very evil and might even kill me and the other fathers and children in the facility." I am listening, but still don't feel quite right. "You want to protect us from that kind of evil, don't you?" he asks, looking at me tenderly.

I feel a deep conflict inside. I don't want to hurt the child, but I don't want Mattheo or the others that I love so much to be hurt. I know all about evil adults, I have met them in setups: terrible people who claw, torture, rape and hurt children and babies, making them scream. Mattheo seems to think that I can prevent this, if I hit this child hard. So, hesitantly, I do what Mattheo asks: I hit the child with a theta blow. The child falls over dead, bleeding from his nose and mouth. It is very much like killing an animal, but with much more sadness.

"Very, very good, Nemesis," he tells me. As Nemesis, I am named after one of the beautiful immortals who has visited my crib since birth. I carry this name proudly because I want to be like her. "I am so proud of you. I love you." He takes me out of the room and plays with me for a whole extra hour that day. I love this extra attention, and know that next time, I will do even better.

By the time I am three years old, I can kill teens and small adults with my theta abilities. I have learned that if I have sexual activity with someone first, it is much easier to create the spiritual connection that will enable the theta killing. There are two other theta controllers along with me, Nemesis, inside: Phobos and Chaos. Along with their systems, they have also learned to do their jobs well. Controllers often come in groups of three. They consider one another "sisters" inside, helping each other to do their jobs well, and also monitoring one another inside for signs of failure which are instantly reported to the programmers.

Phobos has the job of sending dreams of extreme terror to those she visits, while Chaos has the job of creating insanity in those she visits. Phobos has an easy job; she has thousands of terrible memories and feelings of terror that she can draw on from my less than ideal childhood to send out. Chaos takes the memories of being drugged and tortured, and the awful horror she experienced, to send out to others. We three controllers live in a special area internally, with temples dedicated to each of us. When called to present to the outside world, we are treated as "deities", with sacrifices and worship done to us. It is thrilling, but still feels a bit strange, to be called a "god" and to have adults bow to me, but this is part of being an immortal, and I learn to accept it as my due.

Theta training involves training parts to stay in the theta brainwave state. Parts are taught to stay in this state through a course of punishment and reward: punishment for going into a different state, reward for staying in it. The training of theta parts also include much indoctrination regarding the benefits of being in theta state.

Many occultists believe that this is a state wherein the individual has increased spiritual sensitivity and abilities, including the ability to do remote viewing and psychic killing. Based on my adult memories in the cult, the occult societies and government agencies prize psychic killing because the source of the death is completely undetectable: there is no poison, no physical wound, and so it allows an assassination that cannot be explained using physical methods.

Theta state can also enhance physical abilities, such as running faster than would otherwise be physically possible. I have seen individuals walk up a wall and back down when in this state, levitate above the ground, and bend spoons and other objects with their minds. While many in the western world, where logic and scientific "proof" methods have created a worldview that does not allow for the supernatural interventions in the physical world, my own experiences growing up contradict that view.

Spiritual Systems Training

Q'bala Training

I am four years old. I have entered a room that has special black and white patterns, with white and black squares, diamonds and half squares, as well as numbers and runes written on different squares in beautiful white or gold letters. This is a depiction of a part of the Q'bala. I must learn to carefully walk the various patterns and numbers and runes in an exacting, precise sequence. In one of my systems, the Q'bala is the pathway to enlightenment, one which involves learning complex numerical sequences with spiritual meanings.

At the various doors into this room are older children dressed as either a "black angel" or a "white angel". These are the guardians of the Q'bala. They do not allow unauthorized intruders to enter the Q'bala, and at times, I myself play the part of angelic guardian as well, glowering fiercely at anyone who attempts to enter this magical room without the proper codes. I have already internalized this room and am now learning to walk the paths and do complex equations that will provide answers to difficult questions with the help of spiritual beings. I am also learning to internalize my own guardians who are being taught how to do their jobs inside through watching these guardians and interacting with them. My trainers understand that at this young age, an experience is worth more than a thousand explanations, and that the beliefs and behaviors will be internalized much more quickly and longer term if they are experienced concretely. "Experiencing is believing" is their thinking, and I experience many, many setups during my first few years of life.

I am five years old. I am stretched out with arms and legs restrained on a cold, white marble floor. There are demonic beings hovering over each of the points of the sephiroth, special areas on my body which open up portals that enter into the demonic realms. These portals are used for traveling out of body. A special ritual is being done to reinforce the power and to keep open the portal at a point on my upper body. A sacrifice is done, and a bloody baby is laid on top of this area, where it is dying, as I chant the appropriate words.

"Receive this sacrifice, Chokmah", I chant, asking that the entity – an immortal being- that lives in this point of my body will receive my offering to him. I will rely on him and others to help me travel the dimensions, as well as to travel to various locations for remote viewing and other activities. I have been doing this for several years. I barely notice the increased weight and depression as this ritual is done, or how as

Chokmah sits on top of me, he seems to suffocate me. I have been taught that should I do these rituals regularly, that the beings at the points of the sephiroth will take my life if I do not feed them myself in return for their "help" and "power". I do not fail to perform regular rituals to them and have also internalized the rituals: my internal points of the sephiroth all do internal sacrifices on internalized altars, to continue to maintain their power.

The scenes I describe are only a small portion of the cabalistic training that children in the Jesuit order go through. The full training takes years. These memories illustrate some of the terrible feelings experienced by a young child being forced to go through such training. When these memories came back, I tried to get rid of the dark spiritual beings sitting on these points in my body. I knew they were evil and did not want any good for me. However, I experienced extreme panic for several days because the very young parts of me who had gone through these experiences completely believed that these entities protected them. They also believed that these spirits would take vengeance on them or their loved ones, should I ever try to stop being loyal to them. For examples, parts believed that these demons "protected" them from other demons in the dimensions they had traveled. Parts also believed that these demons are able to come from the dimensions and "eat" them if they are not protected, and none of them wanted a creature such as a harpy to come into our dimension and kill them.

It took weeks of grounding and bringing truth to these very young parts to help them realize that we have a protection that is much greater than the power of any demon: the loving authority of the true Jesus. Yes, there were spiritual attacks because the people who had trained me were not happy when they felt in the spiritual realm that something had changed. But at the name of Jesus, those spirits trying to attack me – it felt like a flood of utter darkness and death that tried to enter the room - fled. These spirits were powerless when I cried out to Jesus, and He answered. In fact, when His love entered the room, they were terrified and left. After a few experiences like this, the young parts inside calmed down, and the panic lifted.

Egyptian

I am three and a half years old. I am completely naked and chained to a huge granite statue of Anubis, who has an altar that holds sacrifices between his outstretched arms. I am terrified and trembling. I am in a dark, cold vault beneath a large pyramid structure, lit only by a tiny candle at the other end of the vault. I have been told that I must spend the night here to wait for Anubis. I know all too well that I must please Anubis or he will tear my heart out. I have heard stories about children that did not make him...happy. I am not sure what he will ask and desperately hope it will not be too difficult for me.

It is hours later, the middle of the night, and I am still awake, too frightened to sleep. The statue I am chained to shifts slightly, and then I see it move – literally move – as if it coming to life. It is breathing and talking to me and is asking me a question.

"What did you bring me?" Anubis demands in a low, commanding voice.

I have learned what Anubis requires through careful training. I take the heart of a small child out of the bag I have brought with me, and place it above me, reaching backwards, into his outstretched arms. To my horror, Anubis bends forward and eats the heart. It disappears as he makes terrible chewing noises. Finally, he is done.

"I want more," Anubis says in his deep voice. I place another heart into his outstretched arms, and he consumes this as well. He keeps asking for more, so one at a time, I place the remaining hearts in the bag into his arms, and he repeats this terrible eating. There is a dark, dark presence like a black cloud in the room. I feel terrified and exhausted, as if I have been hiking on a high mountain for hours. This exhaustion intensifies the longer I am in the presence of this entity.

Finally, the red eyes of Anubis turn to me, and he asks the question I dread. "Have you nothing more?" he demands. I know that he is asking to weigh my heart, so I tell him, "Only myself."

"Then, mortal child, you know what to do." Yes, I know, I have been carefully taught what to do, and slowly, reluctantly, with cold sweat dripping off of me, I climb into the waiting arms and lay myself out on the altar.

"Is your heart pure and willing to always obey me?" Annubis asks.

Trembling, I respond, "Yes, my lord."

"Then, I will weigh your heart, and see if you are telling the truth," he says. At that moment, a dark cloud hovers over me, then covers me and seems to enter deep within me. I can feel it probing, seeking, questioning. I feel intense pain and repulsion at this spiritual invasion, but I do not show it or cry out, realizing from my training that to do so would be to anger this being and invite death. I wait in utter fear.

After what seems like a very long time, he finally pronounces, "You are worthy." I have been weighed and found obedient (and frightened) enough. The dark cloud lifts. I am allowed to crawl off of the altar and get down. I have trouble standing or walking, and feel extremely weak and depleted, as if my life force has been sucked out of me. I sit down and the statue changes. Now it is simply a statue and not a "divine being."

After a while, Father Jerome comes into the room. He picks me up, seeing immediately that I am too weak to walk. He puts me into my bed in the room I share with the other children, and brings me a special drink with electrolytes and other things to help renew my strength. I go to sleep while he holds my hand. This special amount of affection and attention is due to his understanding how difficult this ritual has been, a ritual which helps to spiritually install my own internal Anubis, a major controller in my inside Egyptian system. Each child must go through this, and I have heard of some that never return from this terrible room. Fortunately, all of the children in my dorm room pass this terrible rite, and we all are now chained within part of our souls to the demonic spirit that represents Anubis. We will undergo similar rituals for the other Egyptian deities over the next year until we have a full internal pantheon.

I am four years old. I am suspended from the ceiling of a large chamber by hundreds of small golden needles attached to golden wires that have been threaded throughout my body. This is a special ritual for Bel, a Babylonian god. The pain I endure during this ceremony is part of my sacrifice to him. My internal Bel is out, calling on the demonic to help us endure this torture.

It seems as if every cell in my body is in agony, is on fire, as the needles pull and stretch nerve and skin and flesh. Sweat is streaming over my body. After what seems like days, but is only hours, I am finally lowered and the needles and wires are slowly pulled out. I give a special sacrifice to Bel, placing the needles on an altar along with a child I have killed with a golden knife. I feel Bel within me, proud and arrogant, glad that he has shown his strength.

Everyone in the room bows in worship because Bel is a divine being and they are honoring his presence within me. Soon a young girl, my twin sister, dressed as Ashtarte, joins me on two golden thrones at one end of the room. A feast is given in our honor, a meal consisting of wonderful dainties and sweet drinks made of fermented honey. Afterwards, there is a sexual orgy. Many of the adults want to honor Bel with sexual activity with me, his current mortal representative. I am tired, and much, much later, my cult host, who has been called out after the activities are over, climbs into bed and falls immediately asleep. Tomorrow is a rest day, and I am glad, because being Bel has exhausted me emotionally, physically, and spiritually.

Druidic

I am five years old and I am in a remote part of Ireland. My spiritual trainer is with me, and we go into a small forest. The air is very humid with a fine mist. As we walk along a path lined with green, leafy plants, ferns and shrubs, he takes me to an area that is surrounded by very distinctive large rocks with runes on them. Because of my training, I can read the runes: they are a warning to others that this place is sacred to the druids, and outsiders who enter will be killed. Brogan, my trainer, is a druid as well as a Jesuit father, so he can enter this spot and not be harmed. He has been training me for years in the magic of the druids, and signs to me to join him in front of a very large, ancient looking tree in the center of the grove. This tree is huge, at least six feet thick, with twisting, distorted limbs.

I instinctively draw back a bit. I do not like this tree. I have a bad feeling about it. A smell of decay seems to emanate from the moist earth around it, and I have an unpleasant feeling that the tree is watching me. Brogan takes a long, thick rope and ties me to the tree's huge

144

trunk, making sure that I cannot escape. This rope has been anointed with the blood of a sacrifice that we both did before coming to the grove.

"You must spend the night and live," Brogan tells me quietly. This reminds me uncomfortably of the rituals with Anubis and other beings. I realize that this will be a night that I will not sleep and will be tested yet again. "I have full confidence you can do this," he says, smiling at me, but I do not smile back. In some small part of my mind, I wonder why I must go through all of this testing, enduring terrible nights that nightmares are made of. I know I cannot tell Brogan this. Instead, I am silent and pale, and nod my understanding.

"Luce, I wish this was easier for you," he says. "I know this is hard, I do. I went through it myself." It is as if he can read my mind and my feelings, and I realize it is quite possible, with the spiritual bonds between us, that he can. Or, at least, he can pick up on what I am feeling from my body language which I cannot control completely when I am this frightened.

"I will be back for you at dawn," he says. "We will go out for a special breakfast then." I wish that I had his confidence that I will survive. This feels to me like one mean tree, and I don't look forward to being tested by it. I nod and say goodbye, and he quickly leaves.

I have a small canvas bag that contains the required hearts, livers and internal organs that this ancient tree prefers. Brogan has left my right arm partially free so that I can reach into the bag and grab an item as needed. But I cannot wiggle free. I have tested the strength of the ropes already, and I am no match for these inch-thick ropes that have been carefully tied, with the knots far out of my reach.

I sit and wait and wait. It feels like too much of my young life has been spent in waiting on capricious beings, who one moment are smiling and benevolent, but can quickly turn violent, angry, and even murderous. I reflect on how much of the time, our rituals and incantations are spent placating these beings in return for the small favors that they toss our way. Is it really worth it to travel to a remote place and look at documents or to travel back in time, if it means risking our lives or even our sanity to do so?

I think of the poor oracles of Rome, young women permanently chained to pedestals who go slowly insane from their job of giving oracles to all who walk into the dark places, the hidden places of the Vatican. I shudder at the thought. I never want to be an oracle of Rome. It takes a terrible price on the women selected to do so, and I am terrified of these wretched creatures who are chained naked to their pedestals whose hair becomes matted and whose finger and toe nails grow out in strange shapes. I have watched them eat like animals, growling, when they are fed bits of meat, bread and vegetables, or given water from special, dedicated urns, water that is mixed with a bit of blood from the daily sacrifice. I comfort myself with the thought that I have never heard of a child from a top class being assigned by the fathers to be an oracle. If the predictions of my trainers and the older children are correct, I will be in the top class next year.

Hours pass with these and other musings as the night sky darkens. There is no moon and the night is completely black, completely silent, with a growing oppression coalescing in the darkness. Suddenly, I hear a rustle, and a low, sinister voice speaks.

"Who are you child, and why are you here?"

The voice is speaking ancient Celtic, which I have learned in my mage classes. I respond in the same tongue, "I am here to learn from you, and to serve you," as I have been coached to say.

"And what does a mortal child want to learn from me?" the tree asks in a malignant tone.

I shudder a bit, and respond with the lines that Brogan and other mages have taught me. "I want to learn the secrets contained deep in the earth, the secrets of what the wind tells you when it whispers in your leaves, and the secret of long life, from one who has lived as long as you, ancient one."

The tree takes some time before it responds, as if thinking. Finally, it asks, "What will you give me for these secrets? For surely even one as young as you realizes that secrets come at a price – a dear price."

I reach with my one free hand into the bag, take out a child's heart, and throw it up towards the leaves of the tree. I hear a rustling in the leaves, and then a terrible sucking noise. After a while, the tree says, "Ask me one question. If it is a good one, I will answer. If not, I will take your life."

I then ask the tree a question that I have previously been told to ask by Brogan. The tree ponders, then answers me. This back-and-forth goes on for hours, with the tree demanding a sacrifice, and in return, answering the questions I have been coached to ask. Finally, at the end of the night, there are no more questions, and I have run out of sacrifices.

"And what will YOU give me?" the tree then asks malevolently.

I am terrified, and reply, "What do you ask?"

The tree reaches over with one of its woody, twiggy limbs, and painfully, terrifyingly, rapes me with it. I feel as if I am being torn apart inside, and wonder if I am dying. But a minute later, Brogan returns, and the tree stops what it is doing. I look up and see that the sky is turning light in the early dawn.

The tree has turned back into a tree, with no voice, no movement. It is completely, utterly still in the center of this grove where the tree lives.

"I knew you would make it," says Brogan in a hearty voice. He takes a careful look at me, since I don't respond, and places a hand on my shoulder. "I'm going to untie you, and we will leave here," he says.

He unties me, coiling the huge rope into a backpack that he leaves for another to carry out. He then bends, and gently picks me up, realizing that I am unable to walk. I am bleeding between my legs, but the blood loss is not great. It is my mind and spirit that are in shock. I am unable to process what I have just been through and need time to recover from it. In spite of my years of spiritual training so far, this has traumatized me deeply, and Brogan realizes this.

He carries me like a small child in his arms, murmuring, "I love you, and I am glad you made it. I am proud of you." I am glad that I made it, too, and fall asleep, exhausted, as he carries me to a waiting vehicle that will take me to a warm room at a private estate. I will sip hot, sweetened tea and rest for a day before I fly back to Rome with Brogan. A major part of my druid training is almost complete, and I am glad that it is over.

Ancients

I am five years old. I am in a dark part of a large wood in Germany, in an area known for its bogs and huge trees. There is a part of these woods where centuries ago, faces were carved into the ancient trunks of trees. These faces have been re-shaped and chiseled over the years and look startlingly lifelike. Only authorized visitors are allowed in this part of the Black Forest. Intruders kept out by security guards and other measures. A few unfortunate ones end up "stumbling" into peaty bogs where their bodies are sucked deep within, and they are never heard from again.

I am here with Father Jerome to do a ritual before we travel further to some hills. At the hills, we will visit the cave where Grunwald and Grenalyn, two of the ancients, live. I have been taught that these two giants have held up the world since it began. Grunwald goes out daily, seeking prey, to bring back to Grenalyn, his ancient wife who sits continuously stirring her cauldron and adding the flesh and bones of this prey to it.

We travel to the hilly area. After walking around the hills, I shudder as these hills feel forbidding. Finally, Father Jerome and I come to a large cave located on the side of a hill. There is a tunnel-like entrance, and I can smell the unmistakable odor of boiling human flesh wafting out from within the cave. I have smelled it numerous times during my mage training over the past few years. Littered around the entrance, I see the yellowish bones of unfortunate humans who have been caught by Grunwald. I wish fervently that we could leave this dreadful place.

However, I have learned to unfailingly obey my spiritual mentors, and Jerome wants us to be here today. "You are going inside" he says. I look into the dark, menacing opening, and hesitate. I really, really don't want to go in there, but I know that as part of my spiritual training, I must.

I take a deep breath, and enter the low, narrow, dark opening. As I go in, I see the glow of a fire ahead. I hear the hiss of water boiling and steaming, and the sickening smell fills the entrance. I walk more and more slowly, but finally, I am in a large, cavernous cave whose ceiling rises many feet up. The only light comes from a fire beneath a large cauldron, and from a few candles on stone ledges in this rocky room.

There are two large beings in the cave. They look almost like the rock that their dwelling is made of, with huge gray-green arms and legs like bent pillars as they huddle over the boiling stew. They have large, human-looking heads and faces. I can see a few human bones sticking out of the cauldron. The two gigantic figures look at me with malevolent, black eyes that almost glow with hatred.

"Who are you, mortal child?" the larger, male giant asks. "What gives you the audacity to come into my dwelling?"

Trembling, I answer as Jerome and the other mage mentors have taught me. "I am seeking to learn how to become immortal, like you, and have brought gifts to you, for I have heard of your wisdom." Somehow, in these encounters with immortals, I must always be humble, obeisant, and always, always bring gifts; this seems to be a rule of the encounters.

While his eyes are still malevolent, the giant man, Grunwald, looks with more interest at me. "I see that you have been taught by those older and wiser than you, human child," he says. "If they had not taught you, you would be in this stew right now."

A loud cackle emerges from the female giant, Grenalyn, his wife. "As skinny as you are, you wouldn't add much, but it is often the young ones that have the most tender meat." She is sniffing the air, and to my horror, I realize that she is smelling my blood. I act quickly before she decides to pitch me to the stew.

I say, "I have brought you gifts that I was told you might enjoy," as I lift a small infant that is alive and wiggling, in my hands. I hold it towards the two giants, and Grunwald examines it, sniffing it in the same manner that Grenalyn had been sniffing the air before.

"This one has pure blood. It would make a fine addition to our meal," he says. Grenalyn moves next to him, sniffs the infant, and nods. She takes the infant and puts it into the boiling water. We hear its screams that are silenced as it dies. Grunwald and Grenalyn close their eyes in pleasure as the infant is slowly boiled in the thick stew.

"I like your gift, so I will not kill you," says Grunwald. "The infant screamed well before it died. It made a good sound." I am horrified at the pleasure that this giant takes in pain and suffering, and at the same time relieved that I will be allowed to live.

Grunwald then asks, "What do you want to learn about becoming an immortal?"

I respond with the question my mentors had coached me to ask, "How may a human enter the depths of the earth, and mine the precious metal questral without dying?" The fathers know that there are metals deep in the earth that could be used to create the new materials necessary for some of the technologies that they wanted to develop.

Grunwald looks thoughtful, and responds, "A question like this requires an added gift. Do you have one?"

Fortunately, the mages were prepared for this. I bring out a second infant from my bag, which undergoes the same inspection and sniffing as the first one. Finally, both giants nod, add it to the stew, and close their eyes with pleasure as they hear its dying screams.

I am feeling increasingly uncomfortable here, in the presence of these dangerous creatures, and I want to leave as soon as possible. As the fathers want the answer to this question though, I force myself to remain despite the deepening oppression. In spite of the candles, it seems darker in here than when I first entered the cave.

"To go into the earth, you must find the correct gates — you mortals call them portals — and do the correct ceremony to enter," Grunwald says. He then draws a picture on the dirt floor of the cave of the location of the portals which I memorize and will draw later for Father Jerome and Father Mattheo. He tells me the words of the incantation and describes the ritual that will allow a human being to go through the portal and find the treasured metal.

"You must never fail to give a gift to the guardians of the portals, both when you enter and when you leave, or they will shut the doors and you will be buried alive," he cautions. "You must also bring a gift to Teklon, the guardian of this metal deep within the earth."

I memorize his instructions, knowing that the lives of any who attempt this mining depend on my remembering fully and accurately. Fortunately, I have recorder parts, developed and programmed since I was an infant, who can record all visual and auditory details. They will later come out, and share with the fathers everything that they saw, heard, felt, and experienced. I will also share the same, and the fathers will compare what we both say to ensure accuracy.

I turn to leave, and Grunwald says in a deep voice "You are fortunate indeed, mortal child, to be allowed to leave my home. Many mortals come to visit and remain forever." I feel a chill down my spine at the threat in his voice as Grenalyn cackles next to him. I realize that he enjoys frightening me, but it does not stop the instinctual fear that I feel in the presence of this being who I suspect would rather see me dead than alive.

I also wonder, once I am outside the tunnel, where Father Jerome greets me with joy in his voice, why Grenalyn is willing to share this information with me. Why would he give me something that would help us mortals? I wonder. And so, I ponder these and other questions about the metal and the technology that will be developed from it. I wonder if it will really be "good" and for mankind's benefit, as I have been told. These creatures do not seem to want to be helpful at all.

I know that for some, the experiences of Jesuit spiritual training will sound unbelievable. However, to me, these experiences were very real indeed.

These memories are one reason why I talk more about my faith in my recent writings than I had in my original svali posts twenty years ago. As I went deeper into my own healing journey, I recovered memories like these and they filled my little parts with fear. They truly believed that if I remembered, 'the demons will eat us', among other horrors. I needed to find someone, something, that was the direct opposite of these creatures, someone who was loving and could protect me from them.

I found that someone in my faith in the God of the Bible, and His son, Jesus Christ. The kind of love that is caring, protective, and provided the nurture and compassion – and mercy – that I never experienced in the terribly legalistic world of the occult, where rules broken meant death, or at the least, torture. I have been amazed that the true God is not like this at all; that He is not 'performance- based', but instead, freely offered me life.

I would never, ever have had the courage to share these memories publicly otherwise. When I do so, my desire is not to glorify evil, but to show that it is possible to break free from the deepest depths of fear and bondage to such evil. I hope that those from a similar background will recognize that by sharing these things, I am breaking the "vows and oaths of secrecy" that those who become ascended masters make. Yet, in contradiction to their threats and indoctrination, I am alive and less tormented than I have ever been in my life.

I will be honest about having struggled with whether it is okay to break these vows and oaths made during childhood and adulthood. Isn't a promise a promise, and aren't I "wicked and faithless" to be breaking my promises by revealing these things? However, I now believe that these promises to never tell were made under coercion, and these creatures and the adults who coerced my promise to such evil do not deserve loyalty. Promises made to liars who ask for them for evil purposes can and should be broken.

The beings I encountered were universal in their desire for sacrifice, obedience, and worship. They were trying to pre-empt a god role from the human beings (like me) who foolishly sought their "help" or to converse with them. The story I am sharing is the result of this misguided belief, passed on through generations of the Jesuit Order and other occult societies that these fallen angels want to help humans. No, they do not! They only want to destroy human beings, I can say this completely and unequivocally, based upon my own encounters.

The question will be raised, "But can these demons really take on physical form?" I only report my own experiences. I do believe the Bible also illustrates this possibility in its accounts of angels taking on physical manifestation that are visible to human beings with their natural eyes. Examples include when God was sharing his plans with Abraham regarding Sodom and Gomorrah, the angels who physically manifested when rescuing Lot and his family from destruction, and the chorus of angels that were seen and heard in Bethlehem two millennia ago, declaring the birth of Jesus to shepherds. If good angels who are not fallen can manifest, why shouldn't fallen angels also be able to? These are just some issues for thought that I am raising here; I am not a theologian. Most importantly, however, I have come to believe in a loving God whose authority is greater than the evil I encountered as a child. He is more than able to send them away with one breath, or through one word spoken by a believer in the true Jesus with His authority.

I am now going to address the issue of alien encounters as a possible interpretation of these experiences that I have shared. I do NOT believe that these creatures are "aliens". I do realize that beliefs on this topic can differ greatly, and I am only sharing my own belief. I do not believe that these are a technologically advanced, evil race that is enslaving mankind. I have encountered them, and they are spirits, demons or fallen angels who have tried to turn mankind against the true God of the Bible. I am aware that people have memories of encounters with aliens. I do have memories of meeting "aliens", being abducted by them, being invited to visit them, and so on. However, these memories have always eventually been revealed to be staged trickery: studios that were the 'alien spaceships' and the aliens I encountered were cult members dressed in costumes. In my programming, these alien memories were installed as a smokescreens or distractions to 'real' cult memories, i.e., if presenters started to have any cult-related memories that they did not immediately deny or forget, they were then supposed to attribute the memories to 'alien activity'.

Theo

I am three years old. I am sitting on a stone bench in a beautiful indoor garden located near the Vatican.

Although we call it the Vatican Garden, it is located outside of the Vatican itself. It is large and filled with trees, shrubs, and flowers, and sunlight filters down from a large glass roof above. I love it here, and the sweet perfume of the flowers fills the air.

Mattheo has brought me here and has told me to wait on the bench. He leaves. A short time later, an extremely handsome young man appears who looks like he is in his early 20s appears. He is dressed in a black tuxedo with a snow white shirt and black tie, a top hat, and white gloves. He sits next to me and takes off his hat. His jet black hair comes to a widow's peak at the top of his forehead. I know who this is because I have had glimpses of him before at various times during the past few years. This is Theo, the beautiful form of Satan; I know that he can also take on a hideous, frightening form during rituals.

"Hello, Lucient," he says with a smile. I smile back. He is charming and quite seductive in a strange way that has nothing to do with sex. I feel his fascinating attraction. "I'm glad that we can meet together today." I love this special attention and smile some more. "You do know, don't you, that you are very special to me?" he says. "You are very gifted, and one day you will do great things for me." He pulls me towards him and gives me a kiss on my lips.

Then, he releases me. Suddenly, beautiful glass bubbles that reflect the light in rainbow colors appear in his hands. I am awed and amazed, as effortlessly, he juggles these bubbles, first one, then two, then three, four, five, six. They float up, then come down, seeming as light as soap bubbles but much sturdier. "Would you like to touch one?" he offers.

I eagerly reach out and touch the glass, it is so beautiful. I wonder how he can possibly juggle them without a single one falling or breaking. I have seen juggling before, but nothing like this, as these delicate, shimmering objects continue to seemingly float gently upwards and then down.

Theo then turns around and juggles the glass objects behind his back! He doesn't even need to see them to juggle them! I am mesmerized as I watch. Finally, he stops and lets me hold one in my lap as we talk.

"Lucient, I will be asking you to do some very hard things for me during the next few years," he says. His teeth are very white and his skin is pale. He is very handsome and somehow endearing to my heart, which wants to be loved. His look is very loving.

"At times, you won't understand what I will ask, but can you believe that I love you, and want what is best for you?"

I nod. Yes, I can believe him, although I feel a bit uneasy as well, for a reason that I can't quite define.

"Will you show me that you love me?" he asks. Suddenly, I know what he wants.

On the stone paver in front of him, I kneel and bow down, and worship him. He places his hand on my head, and then gets up and disappears. He vanishes into thin air, and I wonder if I have been dreaming. But next to me, on the ground, is a small glass object that reflects the sun like a rainbow. I pick it up wonderingly, and take it to Mattheo who is in his private office.

Mattheo seems pleased. "He favored you with a gift," he says. "I will keep it safe for you here." He unlocks a cabinet in his office and places the glass ball into it. He and I both know that until I am a father, I am not allowed to keep anything that I own, except for medals and a candle, in the dorm room which I share with other children my age. I am happy, because Mattheo is happy, and he takes me out for a gelato, spending special time together as an added reward.

Satan's Throne

I am just a few months older, and I am in the room beneath the Vatican, on a level securely hidden from public access, where Satan's throne is located. The elevators to this level are carefully hidden. No one

162

without using the correct biometric security and codes, which are changed daily, can enter here.

It is many, many levels beneath the public areas. I have visited here before many times during the past three years, watching as penitents and those seeking favors crawl on their knees across shards of glass in order to approach Satan on his throne. He demands this type of act, supposedly to show humility and how much a petitioner really wants what they ask for. Sometimes, he changes the approach to his throne, putting hot stones there, and other objects that inflict pain.

Many people come to this throne room, accompanied by the fathers, including world leaders, and heads of occultic organizations. They line the walls of the room, waiting patiently.

Today is different from the other times I have visited this place. I am sitting in Satan's lap, on the huge, golden throne at the end of the painful pathway. Satan is in his hideous form, and is huge, dark, and frightening in appearance.

A petitioner, a government head, comes towards the throne. He brings a large heart-shaped ruby and a human heart in a golden casket. On his hands and knees, bowing, he opens the casket, and says, "I have a petition to ask, master."

Satan takes this act of worship and the sacrifice as his due. He enjoys watching people groveling before him, and enjoys the numerous sacrifices done earlier in the day to please him before his appearance. Sitting on his lap, I feel this pleasure, too. I am half hidden in the dark, almost cloud-like density of his being.

"What is your petition?" I hear Satan think it, but it is my mouth that opens and voices the question. It is as if Satan and I are someone joined, and I can speak what he is thinking. It feels odd, somewhat filthy, but also very powerful, and very confusing. I am a small child, but here is a leader of a country listening to me because I am representing Satan to him.

I am not the only child to do this. It is part of our training in the Order. This is considered a huge honor and an important responsibility. The fathers have prepared me over the previous weeks for this day, helping me to do the required sacrifices and teaching me how to prepare myself to be a "worthy vessel". Even though I am still young, I am advancing in my theta and omega training, and the mages feel I am ready to do this.

The petitioner keeps his head down, and asks, "I would like to see the downfall of a major enemy." He mentions a warring faction in his country, one that would like to put him out of leadership. "I would like these individuals who are its leaders put to death in a way that makes them an example to the other members of his faction."

This is not an unusual request. People come to Satan asking for wealth, wisdom, and other things, but the most common request is power, whether that power is political, spiritual or in another realm of influence. I have seen church leaders come here and bow, as well as men and women of all ages. The one common thing is that they are all willing to painfully crawl before Satan, bow down, and bring him a sacrifice. Without fail, they are all occultists of a high degree, who are familiar with this dark spiritual reality and willing to pay the price – part of their humanity – in return for a favor.

I listen intently as the man speaks, then hear a whisper in my head. "What do you think should be done?" Satan is asking me what I think. I am surprised and a little terrified. What if I make a mistake? "Give him his request, in return for a yearly tithe of money and people, including children," I think back.

"Very good" Satan thinks in my head. Then, he is thinking very loudly indeed, and the words come out in my childish voice in unison with his. "You will be granted your petition, but on one condition: I require a yearly tithe of your income, which can include the price for young children who can be brought to me instead of part of the money," I proclaim in a loud voice. "Do you agree to this demand?" The petitioner nods his head, and then says softly, "I agree."

He turns around, still on hands and knees, and crawls back to the wall to stand next to the other petitioners who line it. Not all will be seen today, and many will return another day. One after another, Satan and I listen and pronounce his judgments and thoughts regarding each.

By the late afternoon, I am weary and feel that if this goes on much longer, I will faint. It would not do to faint off of Satan's throne, but it is very, very hard and very, very horrible to sit here engulfed by him. I am fascinated that these world leaders are coming and bowing and crawling to Satan, but I am also sick of doing this.

Suddenly, Father Mattheo, who is a top general in the Jesuit army, announces that there will be no more petitions, to my great relief. The petitioners lining the walls bow, and leave, with quiet dignity. Mattheo beckons to me, and dazed, I get off of the large golden throne, and go to him. He holds me in his arms in a hug, and takes me to his private office, where I will lie down on a couch and be brought a meal of soft puddings and liquids. All the while, he is telling me how proud he is of me, how much he loves me. Even so, I feel so very dirty inside, completely defiled. I wonder if I will ever feel clean again.

I understand that these experiences will sound unbelievable to some. Satan appearing in the form of a beautiful young man and talking to a young child? Satan appearing in a hideous form, sitting on a regular basis on a throne under the Vatican? Seriously? I am only sharing what I saw and experienced here. But as I noted previously, I do believe that demons can manifest physically at times especially in situations where they are receiving worship and other things they love best, such as seeing human beings tortured and killed. Whether this was actually "Satan" or another spirit sitting there could certainly be debated, though.

What I do know is that these creatures are absolutely cruel, and their desire is to use people to accomplish what they want on the earth. This includes infiltrating the highest levels of governance in many areas. Demons cannot destroy mankind without mankind's cooperation, which is what they are trying to gain through the misguided obedience of the occultists around the world. This type of evil only has power when people seek and submit themselves to it. When people say "No!" to it and place their faith in the God of the Bible and His Son, these dark creatures lose all power. They are then thwarted in their plans. THIS is why I talk about Christianity so much on my blog and in my interviews. I want people to know that regardless of how evil on earth tries to manifest, God is the answer who brings freedom from the fear that this type of experience can instill in children and adults.

Chapter 5: Other Memories

Being programmed to be a 'presenter'

From early infancy, the programmers created and trained a specific group of parts: the presenters. These are parts that are tasked with presenting in various countries outside of the facility. The fathers design the 'life story' of each presentation according to the needs of the cult. They decide which countries the presentation will live in and where, who their 'families' will be, and the presenter's personality traits and abilities. For instance, while my cult host was extremely athletic, my American presentation was programmed to be clumsy and slow, and to completely believe that she was naturally clumsy and slow.

Presenters are carefully programmed to have no memories of cult life, and to only have memories of an ordinary life with no cult activity in the respective families and countries that they lived in. They are also programmed to be unaware of other parts, and to believe that they are the entire person. Presenters enable the cult-raised, dissociative person with many parts to seem like an ordinary non-dissociative person when interacting with people outside the cult. Alice in

Wonderland programming (see chapter 3) is one of the main programs used to control the presenters.

Presentation parts are created through trauma. The programmers than carefully provide the experiences that will teach each presenter part their 'identities' and 'lives' in their respective families and countries. "Rooms" are set up in the programming studios that look just like the rooms in the houses that the presenter will eventually live in with their 'family' in these countries. The cult members who will play the 'father', 'mother', and siblings' of the respective presentations will interact with the respective presenters by name in these rooms. These experiences create early memories of being in these 'families' for the presenters. Various normal, culturally appropriate family scenarios common for babies and toddlers, e.g., first birthday cake, are staged and photographs of these events are taken. These activities build an authentic seeming life story with evidence such as baby photographs for the presenters. The cult creates complete cover biographies for each presentation in their respective countries.

A very important part of presenter programming is teaching them to only have the abilities (e.g., language skills) that would be expected for a child from that country. For example, when an American, Canadian, or

UK presenter was out, I only heard and was allowed to speak in English with the appropriate accent for that country. If I spoke Italian, Latin, French, or German in an English-speaking presentation, I was tortured heavily, and then sent to "hell", staged scenarios where again, I would be tortured. In this "hell", the presenter would be told she had caused the whole system to become more mortal and less immortal, or to "descend". I felt absolute terror as a presenter in these "hell" scenes, and was relieved when "Satan" or another "divine being" would come and rescue me upon my promise to never forget again and to accept a demonic spirit to ensure permanent barriers between systems. The divine being (an older cult member dressed in a costume, but at times, what seemed to be a real spiritual entity when I was older) would then take me to an altar to do a sacrifice and escort me out of "hell" and back into the presentation setting.

After a few terrifying experiences of "hell", I never forgot again. I have lived with a lifelong fear of going to hell while in my presentations. I could never quite understand this, since the presenter families I was raised in were not religious. All the presentations, including the American, UK, French, German, Russian and Israeli ones, went through such programming until the amnesia barriers between presentations were complete. Presenters are even programmed with amnesia barriers to prevent them from dreaming about one another, or seeing one another's dreams during sleep. Upon hearing special tones, seeing a specific code pattern, and seeing visually one of my primary trainers, I could switch out any of the nationalities desired, and this part would have absolutely no knowledge that I had fathers, mothers, sisters, brothers, aunts, uncles and friends in other countries.

At the age of three, I began being hosted and living in these various families around the world for two or three weeks at a time each year, rotating presentations with three or four other Jesuit children who looked just like me, genetically identical sisters, including Lizzie. These children had been programmed with the same presentation as I had, and were capable of looking and sounding like the cover person they and I were supposed to be in each one. It helped that many of my programmers in the group I was infiltrating (the Illuminati) were also Jesuit fathers, and so they were able to help maintain the cover. In order to maintain the cover when needed, the families would sometimes have an infant or toddler that looked like me to live with them in the presentations before my own hosting started proper at three years old.

While I lived 12 weeks a year in several different presentations, rotating through various presentations and countries as commanded to by my trainers, I always spent most of the year in the facility in Rome. This is what I considered my real "home". This is where my main host Lucia (the cult host) could relax and be myself the most, and where I was able to see my twin brother and sister, my classmates, and the fathers I loved most. Because I was dissociative, I felt no confusion. When a French, Israeli, or other presenter was not out, there was no felt loss of time for several reasons. They had learned very early on to go and stay in Wonderland (see chapter 3), in the area where the presentation language was spoken (overseen by "Alice", a strict controller, along with various punishers such as the Jabberwocky).

It can be difficult to understand how parts can be hosted in different countries, while still spending most of their "real" (cult) life in a facility or occultic training school. This is one reason why the Jesuits raise several children at a time who look identical, who have the same presenters programmed into their system. Having several children who look alike at one time is not difficult for the Order to produce due to their genetics program. For instance, the Order would have four children who are capable of presenting as 'Jane Dupont' (not a real presenter name) in Virginia, USA. They carefully schedule where these children will be at any time, so that there can be one child in the presentations when needed, while the others are in the cult facilities or other places. The other children will be given 'updates' on what each one is doing while presenting so that the narratives remain seamless between the different children with the same presentations. For these updates, the presenters are called out in the labs and watch videos of what the other children programmed to have the same presentations were doing when in France, Italy, etc., in order to add their memories to their own. They are programmed to believe that these videos are their actual memories.

Many highly organized occult societies also have more than one presentation for each person and use twins or other lookalike siblings to cover the presentation roles. For instance, members of the Illuminati are also often programmed to present in several countries, such as the United States, Germany and France. As they know that the same child or twins are playing these multiple roles, the Illuminati would only expect the child or the other children to be in one presentation at a time. E.g., one twin may be at a training facility while the other is presenting in France as an 'ordinary child', while the German and USA roles are left empty for the time being. Because everyone in these children's families is also cult-involved, the parents or family friends in Germany and the USA will not even notice that the child is absent and will have 'memories' of the child being continuously there.

This made it simpler for the Jesuits when they were infiltrating the Illuminati because they would only need to schedule for a child (or their identical siblings) to be in one Illuminati presentation at a time. Their identical siblings can then be in training at the cult facilities or in other non-Illuminati presentations at the same time. But even when programmed to have parts that present in other countries, always the child will believe deep within that their real life is at "home" – the cult training facility.

Learning to do sacrifices

One part of the training that we all underwent, starting very young, was to do sacrifices properly. There was a science and an art to it, and since earliest infancy, our little hands had been led by adults in the proper procedure. By the age of three, we had to be able to hold a ritual knife correctly and stab a sacrifice in the proper spot without hesitation. As we got older, the expectations became greater, until by age ten, we could do all the sacrifices correctly for a major ritual, including skinning and torturing the victim when required.

But there was another type of sacrifice that was especially horrifying, one that was used as a severe punishment.

I am three and half years old, and have disobeyed Mattheo again, making him angry. He had told me to torture a homeless person to death by peeling off all of his skin. This is part of my training in torture methods, and I must learn this and other methods of torture if I want to join the Torturers Guild when I am older, fathers who are highly respected for their skills in torture. For some reason, today I was sick of hurting others, and in a rare surge of saying what I wanted, I said "No!"

This was unthinkable, of course, and I knew that I would be punished, and would probably go to hell for my disobedience. Guilt flooded me, but I still refused to pick up the skinning knife. Mattheo commanded me to torture the man again, and then with rage in my eyes, I did not skin the homeless man; I stabbed him through the heart, ensuring a quick and much more painless death than he would have endured if I had skinned him. But I was also looking Mattheo in the eyes when I stabbed the man, and he saw the unspoken meaning in my act.

Now, I knew I was in real trouble, but if he killed me, so what? I was sick of hearing people scream in slow, agonizing pain. I am trembling inside but struggled not to show it.

Instead of physically punishing me, Father Mattheo takes me into another part of the training school, to a room that contains the small children who are considered "expendable", those used for various rituals. "I want you to find a child that looks like you. I will make you come back for two others if you don't do this," he says.

I go into the room, filled with children in cages, and after looking, I see a three-year-old with brown, curly hair and brown eyes. While not exactly like me, she is the closest I can find. I take her out of the cage, talking softly to her, and lead the terrified little girl by the hand down the hall. She and I follow Mattheo down a corridor into another hall. In the center of the hall is a large, round pit covered with a metal cover. I feel sick inside. I know what lives down deep inside that pit and I taste the bile in my throat that rises.

"Take the cover off," Mattheo orders me.

This time, I obey. I slide the cover off. I can hear the noises from below: first a loud rustling noise, then a chorus of squeaks that send chills down my spine. Down below, the pit is filled with rats specially bred for largeness of size; rats that are hungry. Rats are one of my prime terrors, instilled in me as an infant when Father Carlotti had held a rat over me, and let it bite my hand. This terror was reinforced over the past three years with upsetting scenarios.

I hate rats, and this noise fills me with an unspeakable horror.

"Throw the child down into the pit," Mattheo tells me.

I hesitate, but I know that if I do not, I will be lowered into the pit and the rats allowed to scramble over my feet and bite at me. I can't endure that thought. I push her in and she falls in screaming. Her screams continue as the rats scramble and crawl over her. The screams go on and on, until suddenly they are silenced.

"This is what happens to little children who disobey" Mattheo says sternly. "She paid the price for your sin today; but if you sin again, you will have to go into the pit yourself."

I feel shaken with horror and guilt at the thought that my disobedience has caused another child to die in such a terrible way. I feel despair as I realize that I would not say "No" to skinning someone again. My lesson has been learned: there are worse horrors than hearing someone scream.

What made the lesson especially difficult is that Mattheo was a father figure to me, the person I loved most on earth; whose love and attention I craved. Confused, I wonder how such a loving and wise man could force me to do an act like this. He lets me go, and I am given two hours off to think things over, before returning to my regular training schedule.

That night, I have nightmares about squeaking rats trying to climb up out of a pit, rats that want to bite me. I wake up screaming, and Mary Margaret, who sleeps in my dorm room, comes into my bed and holds me for a while.

Learning to Play Chess

I am five years old, sitting in a large, cushioned chair. Across from me sits one of the three fathers I love best, Father Jerome. He is teaching me how to play a special form of chess. While I already know how to play a basic game, he, an accomplished chess master, is going to work with me on my spiritual training at this special chessboard.

First, he sets up the board, using beautiful pieces carved from pure white ivory and pure black onyx. The kings look like real kings, the queens are beautiful royal ladies in long dresses; the knights look like medieval knights, the pawns like young pages, and the rooks like hunched creatures.

Jerome warns me, "Be sure not to touch any of the pieces while we play." I am an obedient pupil and watch as he uses his mind only to move one of the black pawns forward onto the next square.

"Try to do this, but only move a white pawn. The white pieces are easier to control than the black ones," Jerome tells me. "Use your mind and think about the pawn moving where you want it to go. Be sure to only try to move it one square."

I try to move a white pawn. One budges, edging forward. Excited, I realize that I can play this game, too. Without caution, I try to move other white pieces.

Suddenly, the white king, queen and knights turn around, snarling at me, and fly towards me, attacking me.

I scream as they lunge at my throat. I can feel the terrible pain of their biting and scratching me with their sharp, cold edges. I hear a command, "Stop!" from Father Jerome. The white pieces stop and go back to their places on the board.

I feel shaken and terrified. I realize that this game is dangerous. "It is very difficult to control the pieces, especially for those without much training," Father Jerome warns me. I have already experienced this fact. "Never, ever attempt to try something for which you are not spiritually prepared yet," he says. "This game is part of your mage training and will take great work, and concentration and practice to do well. One day, you will be able to control all pieces on the board, even the black ones." I listen to the rules that I will follow, in order to avoid attacks like the one I just suffered.

Jerome continues, "You are only to play for the next few years with my or another father's supervision". I readily agree, having seen what can happen if I can't control these pieces. Jerome then takes all the white pieces off of the board except for one white pawn and says "We will start here." At the end of an hour, I can move the white pawn one square in any direction, and he praises me. It has taken all of my concentration to learn to do this. I feel exhausted, physically and mentally.

When I am older, Father Jerome will teach me to play a full game. The winner can then ask the chess board a question, and the answer will light up at the end of the winner's side, in silver or gold script. This is considered a high form of mage craft which will take me many years to learn. But one day, I hope to become an ascended master like Father Jerome and playing this game is part of the training process to become one.

The German Father's House

My programming was also intended to help me infiltrate the Illuminati. My biological mother was a Jesuit whose roots were with the German Illuminati. In fact, she was the mistress of Philip Battenberg in Germany for several years. In my cover story, I was his illegitimate child. Therefore, I spent holidays and high ritual days in Germany. I rotated this role with Lizzie and two other sisters, with my mother and others in the Jesuits helping to cover for my occasional absences with plausible explanations.

The Battenbergs were cold, sadistic people and I hated going there. I was called "the bastard" by the legitimate children, who felt that I was permissible to abuse and torment, but not to actually kill. Nonetheless, I had to talk my way out of several close calls as a child.

They had a large, dank, cold basement area under their family castle that was enormous, with a large medieval looking stone altar at one end. I was forced to participate in the rituals and had been carefully coached on how to survive my visits there (and not end up being fed to these demons by the members of the family) by the fathers, prior to my visits.

I remember being very young, about age three during one visit. My biological mother was dressed in a designer gown, looking beautiful, just before a large ballroom event. She let me watch as one of the family came and opened up a huge walk-in vault containing the family jewels, using biometric security. The dark blue velvet casings covering each wall were filled with necklaces, bracelets, pendants, earrings and other jewelry made of diamonds, emeralds, rubies, sapphires, pearls and other jewels. She put on a brilliantly flashing diamond necklace and matching earrings for the event. Later, I peeked over the stone bannister leading downstairs and caught glimpses of the men and women dressed in formal wear. Ladies were in flowing dresses and men were in evening suits, while they danced to a live orchestra. The women looked like exotic butterflies as they were twirled around.

I am just a few weeks older. The night before there was a terrible ritual, and I decide to run away. I want to escape this terrible house. Since I am still quite young, my running involves fleeing into the woods that surround the German father's (Philip's) castle, running over fallen leaves, going down a stream, and then going up to the opposite shore and hiding up in a tree. I hope that the piney branches that I am sitting behind will hide me.

Within a few hours, I am missed. I can tell because I hear the sound of dogs baying and the voices of the German father's servants as they search for me. I am trembling, heart pounding. But the dogs pick up my scent, the servants find me, and they drag me back, shaking and upset at being found. I am thrown down at Battenberg's feet.

"Never, ever run away" the German father tells me in a cold, quiet tone that brooks no disobedience. "I will show you why doing this is a very bad idea."

He then takes me outside where a child my age has been tied to a tree at the edge of the woods. He takes a golden whistle hanging on a golden chain around his neck and blows an eerie pattern on it. Within a few minutes, large silver and black wolves come running up.

There is something strange about these wolves. They have red, oddly intelligent eyes.

As the German father and I stand there, he gives a signal with his hand, and the wolves bound over eagerly to the child that is tied up. They tear into the screaming child with their fangs and sharp claws. The screams continue for a time until they are silenced. The wolves continue their gruesome meal.

Afterwards, to my utter amazement, the wolves stand up on two legs, and turn into young men who salute the German father, and then walk back into the woods. "I have special guards over my property" he explains to me, "very hungry guards." I am stunned, as I contemplate the unbelievable scene I have just seen. "You are very young and foolish, so I will let this pass this time," he continues. "But should you ever try to escape again, I will call my wolves to take care of you." As I look into his eyes, I realize that *take care* really means *kill*. I never tried to run away from the castle again.

I am just a bit older, around four years old. I have been carefully tutored for the past year in etiquette and how to act like a "little lady" by a strict German tutor. Today, I am allowed to sit at the table with the German father and his guests. The plates, silverware and even the flower bowls and candle holders are of pure, softly shining gold. At this young age, I feel overwhelmed and anxious, and when reaching for my glass of milk, a glass that is made of beautiful cut crystal, I accidentally spill the milk, and the cup turns onto its side.

There is a horrified silence at the table, as all the guests turn to look at Battenberg, who is seated at the head of the table. He looks at me with rage. "If you act like a dog at my table, you will be treated as a dog!" he yells. He commands servants to come, saying "Strip her and put a collar on her!"

I am stripped naked, and a lavishly jeweled dog collar is placed around my neck. One of the servants snaps a golden, silken cord to the collar. Battenberg looks at me with angry eyes, and says, "For the rest of the evening, you will be a dog. You will stay down on your hands and feet and will be treated as you deserve."

During the rest of the dinner, I crawl on my hands and knees. "Bark like a dog!" he orders, and humiliated, I do so. I know better than to disobey him. "Beg for your food like a dog!" he orders, and I sit on my haunches and beg like a canine. He then throws me a tiny piece of bread, and his guests titter with amusement.

I feel enraged, humiliated, and shamed beyond belief, but do not dare show these emotions in front of this dangerous man. Instead, I play my role to perfection, even wagging my rear to the laughter of the guests. Maybe if I am cute enough, I will live.

After dinner, the German father gives another order. "Bring in the dogs; since she is a dog, she should spend time with her little playmates."

The dogs are brought in, and they sexually abuse me in front of the guests for their amusement. I am feeling sick and faint but cannot show that I am near collapse. Finally, finally, I am allowed to flee to my room in another part of the palace.

Later, when my mother and I are alone, I yell "I hate him! I hate him! How can you stand to be near him!" My mother holds me, and comforts me.

"You are lucky to be alive," she tells me. "Other children your age often do not survive this type of event. The only reason Philip spared your life is that you are my daughter, and I am his current favorite mistress. He knows how much you mean to me." I go still with the realization that I came so close to death this night.

"Never believe that you aren't expendable, regardless of your rank or status," she warns me.

"Always act with caution around these people." Still pouting, I agree. But while I will externally act well, internally I will continue to hate these people who have treated me so badly. This is how three-year-olds think, and I vow one day to take revenge when I am older.

A German Christmas

I am five years old. It is my turn to spend Christmas at the Battenberg palace. Lizzie and my other lookalike sisters are enjoying Christmas at the Vatican. I am outside with other children and adults. A large circle has been tramped in the deep snow, and in the center is a large deer with tan fur, and large brown eyes. The deer is trembling, its eyes wild, but it is carefully tied so that it cannot move, with gold and scarlet silken ropes.

One of the adults dressed in scarlet robes sticks the deer in the neck, and blood spatters onto the cold, white snow in a pumping fountain: the scarlet red against the white is startling, and the snow steams a little as the blood hits it. One by one, each of adults and children go forward, including me. A golden chalice has caught the deer's blood, and we each take a drink from this cup.

Then, the deer is butchered while it is still twitching. Its heart is taken out and cut into small pieces, and we each eat one piece. As I continue watching, one young child, younger than me, is put into the deer in a baptism and rebirth ceremony, with incantations and ritual words chanted by the adults and other children throughout the ceremony. The child looks terrified and sickened by this experience, and I do not envy her the "high honor" she has been shown.

It is later in the day during the solstice, this same year. I am standing with a dozen other children indoors in a room in the German father's castle. This room has a huge hearth, with a log burning in it that is the length and size of a man. As we stand there, a man enters the room, dressed in clothes similar to those seen at times on very old-fashioned Santa Clauses: he wears a long white robe with golden decorations, a white cap with white fur lining, a golden belt, and is carrying a large sack over his shoulder. In his hand he holds a golden scepter.

"I am Father Yule," the white-bearded man with long silver white hair tells us. "I am able to tell which children have been good, obedient children this past year, and which have been *bad* children that don't obey their elders." As he slowly turns around the room and gazes at each of us, looking deep into our eyes, we tremble. None of us want to be the *bad* one, and thoughts of times I resented things my trainers asked of me flit through my mind.

Then, with a shout, Father Yule raises his scepter. A white light shoots out from it, and to my horror, one of the little boys standing near me falls down dead. "He was bad," Father Yule proclaims. We children are all stunned and quiet, not daring to move or speak. "Who will help me put his body into the fire?" Yule asks. I didn't want to do this, none of us do, but we also realize that not doing so would mark us as "bad". We all quickly volunteer to help, and we all help to carry the little body and put it in the fire in the large hearth.

As the smell of roasting flesh fills the room, Father Yule then opens his sack, and gives each of us a small treat such as marzipan, for being *good*, helpful children. He then leaves, to my great relief. I realize that I never want to spend Christmas in Germany again. I suspect none of the other children want to, either. But the choice is not ours. My visits will be determined by the Jesuit trainers who fill the holiday schedules. But I also know that in three more days, I get to fly to Rome and enjoy Christmas there. The German father will be told that I am due to present in America, but Lizzie, my twin, will be filling that role.

Because the Jesuits were infiltrating the Illuminati, I had several Illuminati presentations (United States, France,

Germany). My cover there was that I was the bastard daughter of Philip Battenberg. As an "Illuminati child", I had to spend time with both the French (Rothschild) family, and the German family, as well as build an identity as a skilled trainer in the United States. This ability to infiltrate them was aided by those who had gone before me: my "mother" in the United States was actually a Jesuit father. She had attained a high spiritual rank in the Illuminati. She was also the German father's mistress. Several of the U.S. trainers who worked with me (such as Timothy Brogan) were also actually Jesuit fathers. They could cover for me if I needed to be scheduled to be out of the country for a time, or if they needed to reinforce the strict barriers between my true (Jesuit) core, and the false core and parts created to be my Illuminati systems.

All the occultic societies try to infiltrate each other and learn their secrets. This is a given. What is amazing to me is the century and a half of patient work and development of impeccable identities that the Jesuits have given to their infiltration. This organization is very patient. When I first tried to leave the Illuminati in 1996, they had no idea that I was a Jesuit. Illuminati leadership wanted me not only stripped of my rank and humiliated publicly, but they wanted me killed in front of everyone. But an order from above said "No." The

Jesuits didn't want me to die. I was flown to Rome for reprogramming, since at that time, much of my loyalty to Rome was still intact. But I was allowed to suffer greatly in my American, French and German presentations in order to placate the Illuminati leaders.

Chapter 6: Military and Academic Training

Starting School

I am six years old, and I and the other members of my class are excited on this very special day.

At last, we are going to give up our brown pre-school tunic and leggings that we have been wearing since we were three years old, and graduate to wearing the hooded brown robes with rope belts. These are the robes of an acolyte, the uniform that school-aged Jesuit children wear in the special school located north of Rome.

For years, as a preschooler in my little brown top and leggings, I watched the older children who went to school, grouped in classes of twelve each, when they sat in the dining facility together. They laughed and teased together, did pranks together, and were my heroes. Now, today, I get to wear the brown robe, and start attending the school myself!

At the ceremony later in the day, I and the other children getting ready to enter the school are all together, grouped by class. I am in the first class of twelve children, Dannie and Lizzie are in the second class, and I see others in the third and fourth class looking excited and happy. Father Jerome is on the platform in front of the large auditorium style room, and he calls my name. I walk towards him. He gives me a brown robe and rope belt; the brown fabric is soft in my arms and I carry it offstage. There, I take off my leggings and tunic, and put on the robe that I will be wearing for the next seven years.

One by one, the other children do the same. As we go back onto the stage, dressed in our robes, there is clapping and cheering, first from the older classes at the school, then by the fathers. The older children all look happy that we will be joining them in the school classes. Learning is very, very valued by the fathers, and this advancement to a new level of study is celebrated by all.

I feel proud in my robe, which makes me look like a miniature monk, as I go into the dining area and sit at my new table, a table that is on the side of the room where the "big kids" sit. I see all of the younger kids looking at me and my classmates with a mixture of joy and envy; they can't wait to wear a robe themselves. It represents a lot of hard work and training, to survive the programming and training of the past six years, and this robe reflects this achievement.

In this specialized school, my classmates and I will learn a large variety of subjects, with demanding standards of scholarship required. The courses will range from anatomy and physiology, to surgical and torture techniques; to ancient languages, to history, to political science, to mage craft, to sciences such as physics, and human behavior and psychology. There is also a daily gym period when we learn to climb ropes, do strengthening exercises, learn gymnastics to a more advanced level than before, and learn more advanced martial arts than we did when we were preschoolers.

Our teachers often remind us that we are receiving "the best schooling in the world" and this is believable to us, with our demanding schedule and the extremely high academic and athletic standards. I am greatly pleased to be a "big kid" at last and look affectionately at the younger preschoolers and toddlers. Later that day, I tell one of them that one day, if they are good and work hard, they, too, will be able to wear a robe like mine

Anatomy Class

I am sitting at a wooden desk in a classroom with the eleven other members of my class. I am anxious not to disappoint, so I listen carefully to the lecture delivered by one of the fathers. In front of him is a live human being, a homeless man, who looks bewildered and terrified, not understanding what is going on. I feel sorry for him but suppress the feeling and listen.

"This is the skin, and I am going to peel it away to allow you to see what it looks like underneath." We have already seen flaying at torture rituals and have already learned how to peel the skin off a human being, but now we must learn more: where the veins, arteries, nerves, bones, and ligaments for each section of the body are located, and their correct names. I know I will be tested on this later, and must memorize everything.

The father slowly peels off the skin with a razor-sharp knife; I watch his technique, how he holds the knife, the angle of his wrist and fingers. Next, he slowly peels away the various dermal layers and fat, discussing the various parts such as sweat glands and nerves, until finally he is showing the muscles and ligaments, then the bones beneath. The man has been screaming the whole time during this demonstration, until he finally faints and mercifully goes unconscious. This is also part of our training, to be able to endure hearing human pain.

The other students and I feel green by the end of this class, but we have learned to suppress, cover, and dissociate our feelings to other parts inside. While feeling a bit dazed, we go out later for lunch, followed by the daily half hour of free play. Our thoughts turn away from what we witnessed in this classroom and towards wondering who will make the most goals with a soccer ball after lunch. There is an intense competition going on between two teams composed of various classes. I look forward to seeing which team scores the highest today.

A couple of weeks later, during anatomy class, I walk in and see that there are three cadavers on tables in the middle of the room. My class is divided into three groups of four each. Each group is assigned to a cadaver in order to take turns practicing the careful peeling and dissection techniques we watched during previous classes. While learning human anatomy, we are also laying the foundation for later doing surgery, and also for performing advanced torture techniques, which we know that all members of the Torturer's Guild must master.

The fathers who teach us are very patient, realizing that it will take time for our young hands and muscles to develop the fine control required to master these techniques. At this stage, they praise us for every success, regardless of how small, and we beam at their praise, choosing not to wonder where these bodies we are dissecting came from. Instead, we focus on the positive aspects of our training; after all, it is the "best in the world" as we are told frequently. We should feel grateful, we continually remind ourselves.

During another lesson, all four classes are taken to a glass window of a large freezer for a lesson that will help us understand better how to prevent cold-related injuries when we do missions in cold climates. A homeless man is brought through the door into a freezer that we are told is at a temperature of ten degrees below zero (C). We watch closely as he shivers, and after a period of time, gets sleepy. At one point, while he is still alive, the man is taken out. Our instructor shows us the effects of severe hypothermia on his hands and feet: they have turned a dusky grey color, and he has no sensation in them. "His fingers and toes are dead, because he had insufficient protection," our teacher warns. "Always wear sufficient protective equipment when working in severe cold." This object lesson makes a deep impression on our young minds. I determine to always do equipment checks on my teammates when we do military or other training in cold climates. I don't want myself or anyone else I love to go through this.

This lesson is repeated a week later with an individual placed into an enclosed room at 49 degrees C, without water. We observe first-hand over several hours what happens when a person begins sweating and losing water and electrolytes, and does not replenish them. We all vow to always bring sufficient water and electrolytes with us when training or working in a hot climate.

The fathers who teach us realize that at age six, children are still very concrete in their thinking, and that actually seeing or experiencing these things will make much more of an impression than a lecture ever could. They are very "hands on" in their teaching methods, and these lessons were imprinted on my mind forever in the parts who attended these classes.

History and Political Classes

The Jesuits firmly believe in understanding politics, since their agents will "pull the strings" behind the scenes in numerous countries where they have both a presence and influence. This includes significant influence over leaders around the world (but not all, thankfully!). To prepare the children for future leadership roles on the world stage, they must understand the history, culture, economic and political movements within countries around the world, and the complex factors that drive the leaders of these countries.

In the early years of schooling, we not only heard lectures, but saw re-enactments of famous scenes of history, often put on by the older students as part of their own study, with help from the fathers. These scenes included scenes of key military and political leaders conducting strategic planning for major wars; the intense politics behind the scenes in the early church, both in Rome and Constantinople; the breaking apart of the Roman Empire, and the forces behind this; the feudal systems of Europe, China and Japan; the cultural and religious development of these and other countries, such as Tibet and India. We also studied factors that influence poverty and wealth; the role of tribal culture and ethnicity in the politics and distribution of wealth in various nations, and many other aspects of politics and society.

Part of our training in politics was also learning how to recognize power, such as being able to sit at a table and identify who was the most important person at the table by watching the body language of those sitting. Another skill taught was how to discover the subtle information that can help with gaining influence without appearing to do so. We also learned how to negotiate to gain concessions while leaving those conceding feeling as if they have triumphed in the negotiations. These skills will be practiced for many years, into early adulthood.

As older students, we often accompanied the fathers on political missions as part of our training. For instance, at student might be taken along for negotiations with members of a Muslim nation for oil drilling rights for a key member of the Illuminati, who the Jesuits would be representing in return for an important favor. The Jesuit father would be attended by a ten-year-old student who would stand quietly in a corner, observing, and later report everything they saw going on in the room. The student was told to appear as if they did not understand the language of the negotiators, to smile and nod stupidly if addressed, so that if the father left the room, they could listen and report what was said while they were gone.

Older students would be responsible for packing for these trips and organizing the delivery of luggage and other items. They also checked hotel or private rooms stayed in for "bugs" and bombs, since some negotiations at times occurred in less than friendly situations, and these types of things were anticipated.

I am eleven years old. Father Mattheo, Father Timothy, Father Andrew and I, along with Conner, are staying in a private suite with three rooms in a large mansion in St. Petersburg. It is cold and snowy outside in this bitterly cold Russian city.

Father Mattheo signs silently to Conner and me to do a complete sweep of the room. This is one of the skills that we must learn if we are going to go on missions in other countries. We all joked on the plane over that it is an assumption that they will try to monitor us and learn confidential information while we are in our private rooms.

Conner and I take out our equipment, and check everything in the rooms of the suite, using state-of-the-art technology. After doing the complete sweep, we both identified numerous listening devices which we then brought to the fathers and deactivated. We also found and deactivated a tiny video camera hidden within the beautiful chandelier over one of the beds. I discovered a small bomb located in one of the bathrooms, and Conner found another beneath one of the chairs. We quickly disabled them under the supervision of the fathers.

"Somebody doesn't seem to like us," Conner jokes, and we all laugh. These types of things are to be expected, but even so, the bombs were particularly unfriendly for a group that is supposedly wanting to secretly negotiate with the Vatican. This is the reason for our presence here; there will be no media coverage or publicity as these fathers, all skilled negotiators, sharpen their wits and hold their bargaining chips close to their chests in preparation for the day's meetings.

"Well, this will give them something to think about," Mattheo says. "I will also remind them of what could happen if any of us are harmed while we are here. I think they didn't believe me when I mentioned the need for cordial relations while we are here."

Later, we all walk into the conference room, unharmed and with our private conservations unheard by those we were meeting. I laugh inside to see the look of complete surprise on the faces of our hosts for the meetings. They had not counted on our technology having the capability of detecting and disabling theirs, which took away any unfair advantage they might have brought to the negotiating table. This impressed upon me that one can never be too careful when negotiating with those who are hostile.

Baby Soldiers (Military Training)

The Jesuits start the military training for their children very young, almost as soon as they can walk. Toddlers are taught to stand in a straight line for a few minutes at first, then for longer time periods. Two-year-olds are taught to do short marches together. By age three, the children can march, stand, and practice with guns. They are taught to take apart, clean, and fire small, light guns. By age four, can shoot together at a target on command.

The children are very proud of these accomplishments and I was no exception. I looked with envy at the older children, who by age six were allowed to wear real camouflage uniforms with starting ranks. We were not ranked yet, and our "uniform" consisted of small leggings and a tunic. The older children constantly told us how great it was to be in a real "unit", to do the military exercises, and told us that if we did well, one day we also could do the same.

This peer modeling was a very important factor in our early training. The older children we admired and looked up to, children that played with us at times and many of whom we loved, constantly reinforced performing well in the military training, emphasizing both how fun and how important it was. They even shared some of the pranks they played on the teen leaders with us, to our wide-eyed, admiring stares. By the time I was five, I wanted to be a "good soldier" with rank more than anything else in the world; to be like the strong, brave, talented older "brothers and sisters" who had achieved this already.

By age five, we could march, stand in formation, shoot, and even climb a small mountain with guidance. We were learning to read maps; to use equipment to communicate with each other and other teams and the adults supervising us, in preparation for the real military exercises we would be doing in a few years.

I am seven years old. I am in a hot, dry desert area that has sand everywhere., and I have a canteen of water. My eleven classmates also have water. We have been given a map of the area and terrain and have been told that within 12 hours we need to reach a certain point on the map. We have already learned to read maps and we pull out our compasses (no cheating with modern GPS allowed, the fathers want us to learn to do this the old-fashioned way first).

"I think we should go here first," I point to the left of a large hill in the distance. "That way, we will get more shade than if we try the other side or try to climb the hill."

"I agree," Conner, my second says. "We can take a rest there before we go on."

We look at the other ten. It is important to listen to input from everyone on this team, in case they see something we don't as we plan. This working together is the whole point of this exercise.

"I think it's a good plan," Mary Margaret, my third, says. The other children nod their agreement.

Because we have been doing hikes for years, we are in good condition for children our age, condition augmented by our genetics for increased muscle strength and our excellent physical health. We slog through the sand, which is harder to walk through than a harder surface would be. In spite of seeing the hill ahead, we carefully use our compasses to verify direction. We have been taught that deserts can be tricky, with mirages making objects appear in places very different than the actuality; or they can appear closer than they actually are. So instead of just our eyes, we rely on our compasses as well, checking the readings with each other.

Eventually, after several hours, we reach the hill. We are all sweating, but we have been careful to only drink small amounts of our water in sips. We still have over half a canteen full to get us through the rest of the hike. We reach the shaded side, and collapse on the sandy ground together.

"Boy, it's hot!" Timothy exclaims. "I wish I could pour this water on my head." He and the rest of us know better than to do this, but the thought is tempting.

"Hey, you complained it was cold when we did that hike in the mountain snow a few months ago," Conner teases him, referring to some training done during winter in the alps in northern Italy. "I think you want it to always be a balmy 25 degrees (Celsius)."

"Well, it will be balmy when we get home," I say, thinking of the beautiful weather in Rome this time of year, now that it is late spring.

We each eat a small biscuit that is dense with electrolytes, minerals, protein and other necessary nutrients. We were given the biscuit and put it in our pockets before we started out. Its taste is not unpleasant, and we know that we need to replace some of the salts we have been losing from sweating. This knowledge came from the desert survival training classes that we attended before attempting this hike, including a practice hike for several days with two of the fathers who were dressed in camouflage, like we were.

We learned then that if we need water, there are certain plants to look for that may grow in an area, plants that we can suck water out of, and were able to practice this under supervision. We also know to pace ourselves, and not push too hard in the heat – the reason for this rest in the shade.

After an hour, I get up and stretch. "It's time to keep going, if we want to get there in time," I say. I am leading this hike today; I am the class leader. Conner and the others have also led other hikes and missions, as training to lead others is another important skill to learn. After a quick sip of water, we all get underway, with maps in hand and our compasses ready to guide us.

I enjoyed the military training a lot. It was fun to go outdoors; to learn to purify water; to forage for food, to hike through different terrain, to read maps, to learn to read tracks and eventually to follow a track left by an adult in preparation for the more difficult training once I became older. During this time, I learned to go downhill to look for water; to tell direction by looking for moss on trees and other signs.

At times, I wished that we could do military all the time and not have to do the other training. The only parts I didn't like was having to learn to shoot people and interrogate them with torture; I wish those parts had been left out.

Climbing the Mountain and Teamwork

Each year, my classmates and I were being taught more and more difficult maneuvers, including specialized military maneuvers. We learned how to survive in all types of terrain: desert, mountains, tropical, arctic cold, and moderate climates. I learned how to pitch a tent in a short period of time; how to build a fire using any variety of fuels available; how to use chlorine tablets and filters to clean water, boiling it afterwards to prevent illness; how to identify native plants and animals, and determine which were safe to eat, and which to leave alone.

By the age of ten, I could hike many miles; could climb with a rope and mountain pick up and down a mountainside; was well-trained in the martial arts and could take down adults who were trained in these arts; and shoot well, hitting the target every time. I was also leader of my class, and as such, was responsible for leading them through the training exercises that we were expected to complete as a group. Conner was my second, and marched behind me; while Mary Margaret was my third, and marched in the rear, keeping an eye on anyone who appeared to be in trouble. I had learned over the years to completely rely on them, and they on me, and we worked well together.

I am ten years old. Our class has been told to cross a rope bridge over a high ravine. My classmates are all excellent at these things, and I do not anticipate any problems as we cross, using the two upper ropes to steady ourselves as we walk across the thick bottom. I cross first, testing the ropes and seeing what it is like. This is part of a timed exercise, with two more miles to hike before we reach bravo base, the camp where we will spend the night.

Conner follows, then one after another, they all cross except one. For some unknown reason, John is slow to start crossing. Halfway across, a breeze hits the ropes and he slips, then recovers, but he freezes in the middle of the bridge. I look at him, and realize that he has panicked. "John, come on across, it's okay," I say, in a calm, quiet voice, staring at his eyes from the edge of the gorge. "You can do it."

John is gripping the ropes with tight hands, as if for dear life. He is truly frozen, something quite unusual for this normally extremely brave brother. John looks at me with terrified eyes, and I realize that he simply cannot do what I am requesting.

"John, I am coming for you", I say, as I move onto the rope bridge. I have walked it and know that it can bear both of our weight, by its feel and the thickness of the ropes. "Keep looking at me, and don't look down," I tell him, keeping my eyes on his as I come closer. I then hook a rope to his belt, telling him, "Now, you can't fall; I've got you." I tell him, "Keep looking at me, don't look down," and I back across the rope bridge backwards, slowly, feeling for the rope with my feet, keeping my eyes on John's the whole time. I don't want him panicking and falling, since I can't fully trust that I wouldn't fall into the steep gorge with him. I am literally willing him with my mind to take a step, to not feel afraid, using my theta ability. John takes a hesitant step forward, then another, and I breathe with relief. Finally, we are on the other side; Conner grabs me and Mary Margaret grabs John. We are both safe now.

John explains what had made him freeze: a trauma memory of being suspended over a cliff during infancy was triggered by his near fall. This kind of triggering is highly unusual because of how carefully cult children are programmed to compartmentalize their traumas to specific internal locations. I make a note to let his trainers know, since they will need to deal with this and prevent further occurrences of such bleedthrough memories emerging at the wrong time. I am shaking a bit, since what I had done was extremely dangerous. I know that my military trainers will not be happy with me when they hear about it, since we are not to risk our lives needlessly, but I don't care. I know I have done the right thing and will deal with the trainers' griping later. What is important is that John, a member of my team and my class brother, is okay. We finish hiking to the base, and I go to the company commander to debrief and tell him about John.

I am eight years old. "There will be times when during a military maneuver, in order to save the others in your unit, you will have to leave the wounded behind," bellows a military trainer. I hate hearing this, but know it is true. It isn't right to risk the others for someone who cannot keep going, when there is life-threatening danger.

A few months later, my class and I are doing another training exercise. It is in the mountains, and as we go down a steep, rocky hill, one of my classmates, Paul, slips and badly sprains his ankle. Instantly, the rules of this exercise flash through my mind: "You are all to return to base at the same time. Anyone who does not return within the time limit given will be shot." I quickly assess the sprain; Paul's ankle is badly sprained, possibly broken, on the rocks he had fallen on. "You guys keep going," Paul tells us. "Don't make yourselves late." With a heavy heart, as team leader, I make the decision. "Keep going," I tell the others, and we do.

I never see Paul again. I have to assume that as we were told, he was shot. Another boy from the second class, Mark, moves up to take Paul's place, and I grieve silently, quietly inside for a brother who I had loved. Mark is a great kid, but he is not Paul; but I cover my feelings and embrace Mark as part of our company the next day.

I am eleven years old, and my class is climbing a large mountain. We are competing with two other teams our age; the first class to climb to the top and plant their flag wins the competition and will be given two days of R&R off as a reward. My team and I badly want this R&R, and we are giving this climb all we've got. But this climb is hard! The thin mountain air makes it hard to breathe as we ascend more and more slowly towards the top. I can see the top; it is only a hundred feet away. But my team and I are so exhausted, on shaky legs, that we get onto our hands and knees, and start crawling the last part of the trip up.

I look back, and to my dismay, one of my brothers has collapsed; he is unable to even crawl any further. I go back to him, along with Conner and Mary Margaret. "What's going on?" I ask Jonah, the brother who has collapsed.

"I can't go any further," he gasps. "I can't. I'm sorry, I wanted to win." The rules of this "game" are that all members of the class must reach the top, or they will not win.

I talk softly to Mary Margaret and Conner, and together, we get on our hands and knees, and put Jonah on our backs. "We are going to win," I say, and the other two nod. "We're going to carry you up with us." Jonah tries to make us stop, but we are stubborn, and tell him to shut up and we continue towards the top together.

We three crawl with Jonah on our backs the last 100 feet up the mountain. Each foot feels like a mile, but shaky, we make it, then collapse at the top and plant the flag. Our team lets up a shout, we have won!

Later, when I debrief, the trainers in command of the exercise are not happy. "You aren't supposed to carry teammates up the way you did, that's cheating," they tell me.

"I wasn't told there was a rule against doing so," I argue back. There was indeed no rule against carrying teammates up the mountain, simply because in the past, no team has ever done this before. "I think we showed creativity and teamwork, and isn't that what you want?" I ask. "To teach us to work together to meet a goal? Well, we did; we worked together and all made the top of the mountain."

The trainers tell me to leave and confer together. Later, I am told that my team will be awarded the coveted days off, and I tell them to much rejoicing. We have a wonderful time together in a local Swiss town, sailing on the crystal clear waters of the lake and enjoying lots of good chocolate and baked goods. We congratulate each other on our achievement, then go on to our normal teasing of each other. In many ways, we do act like brothers and sisters, and enjoy this special time to just be children. It is all too easy to forget that we are still children, with the increasingly heavy demands placed on us at this time in our lives. We know that in just over a year, we will be considered adults in the Order, and soon after turning 13, we will go through a special ceremony at the end of which we will be fathers.

The fathers, while strict, also welcomed argument if it was logical and reasonable. When I and other children argued with good reasoning why a position was right, they often agreed. They were usually quite fair when a situation allowed it, and in fact, encouraged budding young leaders in their organization to think strategically and to find unusual solutions for complex or difficult problems. This, too, was part of leadership training in the Order.

Break Time and Pranks

The schooling we went through was very intense. By age 12, in addition to our extensive military training, we had the equivalent of a medical school degree, were able to perform surgery, speak numerous languages, had an encyclopedic knowledge of world history and current events, had the ability to strategize solutions for complex and politically delicate situations, and other skills. But we always looked forward to our daily break after lunch, when we were allowed to play and simply be children. We needed those breaks, and the fathers provided them as an essential way to let off steam and let go of the stress for a time.

During these breaks, soccer, Jai Alai, and other team games were very popular. If I or my classmates had a (rare) full day break, such as after a difficult mission or military exercise, we often went sailing or swimming with close classmates, or had lunch out at a local trattoria, dressed in civilian clothes instead of our usual robes or military camouflage. By age twelve, we were considered adults in the order (more on that later) and began to enjoy more adult privileges.

But we were also children; brilliant, creative children with the ability to strategize and plan, so my classmates and I enjoyed coming up with pranks. For instance, each day in the dining room, a large well-lit computerized board displayed the rank of each class, and of the members of each class, with their skills listed and ranked as well. This was motivational, since everyone wanted to have a high rank, and to help their class hold a high rank.

But on this day, my class had hacked into the computers, and laughter was heard around the room, as the board displayed the names of the fathers (trainers), with their ranking listed, and specific abilities scored, such as charisma, intelligence, and sexual performance. Everyone had fun when this happened, including the fathers who had a sense of humor and an appreciation for the skill it took to hack into the school computer systems to accomplish this.

But my class was still called in, and I was singled out, along with Conner and Mary Margaret, as probable instigators.

"You all seem to have too much free time," Mattheo tells us, hiding his smile. But I see a twinkle in his blue eyes anyway. While he has to discipline us, he has a sense of humor, and will not be too harsh. "Since you seem to be bored, I think your class should stay inside during free time for the next two weeks, and research the use of ancient Sanskrit in poetic form and what it means to you when you read the verses. I want you to also describe how they relate to today's society."

We complete this boring task as requested. But to our great amusement, we also hear the trainers laughing among themselves for weeks about the various rankings, with plenty of teasing for those ranked low in sexual performance, or sense of humor. What they don't know is that our class has previously installed a listening device in Father Carlotti's office, and we have been listening to the other fathers' conversations with this father.

In another school prank, my classmates and I went and switched out the espresso coffee grounds in the labs and school rooms with decaffeinated coffee. Most fathers drank espresso like water to keep them going during the incredibly busy days and large workloads they carried, and we noticed a distinct lag in many of them by the end of the day. Of course, they figured out what was going on, and once again, my class was put on extra work detail for a few weeks.

But even worse, they also cut my class off from all coffee for a week! This was hard on us, since the children are permitted weak coffee starting from the time we enter the school at six years old, and most of us drank quite a bit. We had major caffeine withdrawal headaches for a few days, but after a week, we were allowed our coffee again.

In yet another prank, two classmates and I hacked into the scheduling computer, and gave our class two weeks off in the schedule. Again, this was disciplined, but it was worth it since we loved outsmarting our trainers. The trainers understood the need to "let off steam" and allowed a certain amount of this, as long as we didn't cross the line into outright disrespect or causing harm to another, which was never tolerated.

Chapter 7: Learning to Become a Mage

Jesuit children are taught to become mages and ascended masters, with their training beginning at a very early age.

I am six years old. I am entering a chamber made of stone, and lit by candles made of human fat. This is where we are taught how to be mages by Kalyx, one of our mage trainers. His white hair and piercing gray eyes were formidable, and he spoke to us in gentle tones that differed greatly from the words he was telling us.

"You must always, always recite any incantation that you do in this room with exact correctness, and with the correct enunciation, or something unfortunate will occur." His fierce eyes hold sadness for a moment.

I raise my hand, with a question. We are always encouraged to ask our trainers questions when it seems appropriate, and there is something I want to know. "What do you mean by unfortunate?" I ask, wanting to understand the consequences of an ill-said spell.

Kalyx strokes his long beard which he is allowed to grow since he is older and no longer doing physically active missions where his beard could get entangled and endanger him. All of the younger fathers are clean shaven, but secretly, I think Kalyx enjoys the wizardly image that silver white hair and beard portray to us children.

"I once mentored a child," he says softly, "who was learning a spell to become invisible. He had done the proper sacrifices, and he said the correct words, but he failed to enunciate them correctly. At the end of the spell, he put the accent on the wrong syllable!" He pauses, with a look of horror on his face.

These mages are great storytellers, and the whole class is listening, spellbound, to find out what happened to this child who made a simple, tiny error.

Kalyx continued, "Suddenly, the demon he had been summoning raised up, turned on the child, and ...ate him!" Kalyx gave a shudder of horror at the remembrance of this terrible event.

The jaws of every child in the room fall open in surprise and fear. We are all thinking in unison that we will memorize the correct enunciation of every spell that we will be expected to learn. None of us want to be eaten, and we are primed to study and memorize very well, indeed.

But children can be a bit suspicious of stories like this, without even consciously realizing it. So a few weeks later, when we are in this stone chamber with Kalyx, he tells us, "I have something to show you." His face is white and solemn.

He turns on a screen in the back of the room. "This film was shot in our facility in Poland," he tells us, and the video begins playing. It shows a young child, not much older than we are, who is doing an incantation. In the middle of the film, the child stumbles on a word. With horror, we watch as a large, dark column of smoke comes up from the ground, and strips the flesh off the bones of the child with a loud ripping sound.

We all instantly decide to memorize the spells and incantations we are given with even greater care.

It was not until I was healing as an adult, that I realized that this video could have easily been created using virtual reality or graphics. But at the time, as a child, I fully believed what it portrayed.

At first, the incantations my class was given to learn were quite simple, for things such as creating a small fire that came from our fingertips, or a bubble of blue light, that would follow us around the room, to see with. As I got older, the incantations were more complex, for things such as seeing into the past or the future; or to create invisibility. Many of the incantations involved special sacrifices, and part of the training, which included learning to read the spells in ancient languages, was to correctly identify which beings were to be called on for each spell, and their particular characteristics. It was essential to know what "gift" – the proper sacrifice – was need to invoke them, and the correct thanks to give after receiving answers to a spell. Early on, we learned to draw special circles to protect us from the being we were invoking, and staying within a special circle drawn with precision on the ground for personal safety during some incantations became second nature. We learned to use special drawing tools to draw these circles, and also learned to draw more complicated diagrams as our classes continued over the years.

There was a huge library which the mages and students (only with permission from the mage tutor) could use. When I was younger, I never went there without an adult, since there was hideous looking demons sitting at the end of various bookshelves, guarding it from unauthorized "intruders". There were many of these guardians all around the library, so there was certainly no fear that an outsider would ever get in and use these books.

As I got a bit older, a father who was mentoring me would at times ask me to go into the library and get a book for them from these specially guarded areas. The father would tell me the password to prevent being torn apart by the guardian over that part of the library, but still I trembled and hurried through the task of retrieving the book.

Some parts of the mage library were lighter, with fewer guardians, and contained literature from around the world. We were encouraged to read fairy tales, both ancient and newer, and to read them in the original languages. There were books about ancient civilizations such as Atlantis and others that had been lost years ago, with diaries of those who lived before their destruction. I loved reading these books.

Some books were very special. They were filled with beautiful pictures, and with the right incantation, the pictures would start moving and become extremely realistic-looking, just like a small movie. Other books with gilt letters would begin reading themselves out loud. The mage library was a strange and wonderful place, but one that I always entered with caution.

All children and adults within the facility attended twice daily "chapel". This started during infancy when we were carried in sitting in our little infant seats. But it was not like chapel at most schools. We had an outstanding children's and adult choir that sang praises and worship with beautiful melodies, but these praises were to Satan, not the Christian God. During chapel, we would watch or often help in the daily sacrifice on a small altar in the front.

There was also a daily sacrifice done at the beginning of the day on an altar in front of the programming labs.

During special times of the year, on the highest holy days (Yom Kippur and Passover; the Jesuits follow the Jewish calendar for their highest festivals), the rituals seemed to go on for hours and hours. When I was young, at times, it was hard to stay awake through the whole ceremony, especially after a long day of hard work at school. The voices would drone on and on during the lengthier rituals, and the words seemed to blur together. But I was warned to never, ever fall asleep, since not only discipline would occur, but I was told a demon might eat me. My classmates and I would surreptitiously poke one another to stay awake. We made it through the ceremonies, even as young children, even late at night. But some nights, it took a lot of pokes. Afterwards, we would all stumble and fall into our beds with relief, to fall deeply asleep.

The Elements

The elements (earth, air, water and fire) were involved in numerous rituals and incantations. As part of learning to control them, I had to learn various rituals and spells. For instance, earth was often represented by soil, but also by rocks. When I was eight years old, one part of my training was to be placed under a wide board the length of my body, while rocks were placed one by one on top of me. I felt as though I was being crushed and suffocated; I could barely breathe. At this point, I called out to the spirit over the element earth to rescue me, and then concentrated my mind as well. Suddenly, the rocks flew off of me, and I was able to move, push the board off and sit. Because I lived through this test, I was able to graduate to the next level in my mage training. While I never saw this myself, I had heard that some children did not pass this test and were crushed. These children were considered sacrifices to the element.

I am 11 years old. I am floating on a raft in the ocean. I can feel the hot sun beating down on me, with rays that feel hot and dry. In a cage is the live sacrifice, a baby, I have been given in order to survive this ordeal. I am thirsty, my tongue feels like sandpaper in my mouth, and I am thirsty, as I speak the incantation to draw Kraken, the keeper of the sea and one of the water element guardians, to the surface.

After what seems like hours, there is a boiling of bubbles in the water near my raft. I feel excited, but also afraid. I am not sure what will happen since elemental guardians can be a bit unpredictable. Hoping that Kraken will be in a good mood, I wait. Finally, a huge monstrous creature that looks like a giant squid, with flashing red eyes and long fangs, rises out of the water, accompanied by a whirlwind of water. It towers over me. I smell rotting flesh and seaweed in a sickening mixture.

Terrified, I scream. Then, as the monster comes closer to me, I remember the words of the ritual, and incant "Please take this sacrifice I offer as a symbol of my deep desire to serve you" in an ancient language, while I quickly open the cage. The monster pauses and opens its large mouth. Quickly, I throw the baby into its yawning black orifice. The monster sucks and drools and chews, then it deposits what looks like a large pearl on my raft. It then turns and slowly, slowly it descends into the deep water.

In spite of shaking hands, I have never paddled a raft as fast as I did now, going back towards a waiting boat that is nearby but not too near, since the others waiting are aware of how malicious and unpredictable the Kraken can be. Once I am hauled on board, I continue to shake for an hour from adrenaline and shock, glad to be alive and hoping that I will never have to meet this creature again.

Later, I take the pearl to Mattheo and Jerome.

"Hold it in your hand and ask it a question you want the answer to," Mattheo tells me.

I do so. I ask it who my worst enemy will be when I become a father. To my surprise, the pearl glows, then gives an answer. Then, the pearl slowly fades away. This answer was Kraken's return "gift" for the sacrifice I had brought it.

For fire, at the age of nine I was taken to an ancient volcano site where molten lava poured into deep crevices; after summoning a fire creature out of the lava, I gave a sacrifice. I was then able to walk over nearly molten stones. At the age of seven, I had already gone through a ceremony where I had done numerous sacrifices before being placed in a golden chair. I was then carried and placed into the midst of a fire for several minutes, then carried out. This was a "passage by fire" ritual that each of us children had to undergo and survive, as part of our training.

When learning to control air, I was taken into a desert and was taught to do rituals and sacrifices to summon up winds and then sandstorms, taking shelter in nearby caves until the storm passed. I also learned to create a thunderstorm with lightening as a young teen, as part of my mage training.

Traveling Dimensions

One part of mage and ascended master training involved learning to travel the dimensions. This began at a very early age, with the youngest children learning to travel accompanied by a father they loved to the first dimension at around age two and a half or three years

The age at which a child begins travelling depends on the assessment of their readiness. This dimension looked a bit like a fantasy world, with bright-colored flowers that talked, animals that talked, and unicorns and other mythical creatures that the child could ride while exploring the dimension. But these fantastical flowers and animals had a malevolent side, as well.

I am two and a half years old. This is my second journey to the first dimension. I was able to travel there with Father Mattheo who held my hand while we traveled. He had cautioned me to always hold his hand during the journey there and back to ensure that I could find the way back to my body which was lying on a small bed in the facility.

I think this place is beautiful. I feel fascinated by its wonders. The flowers are singing, and I walk away from Mattheo in order to smell one and talk to it. I am quite a distance from him, looking at, listening to this wonderful scene.

Suddenly, the flowers are all yelling at me. They begin stabbing me with sharp, hard petals that hurt. "Bees, bees, come here!" one blue flower with big eyes cries out. I see and hear a swarm of bees start to come towards me, with a loud buzzing noise.

Terrified, I cried out "Mattheo, Mattheo, help me!" Suddenly, Mattheo is at my side. He grabs my hand and escorts me back to the portal that we came through to enter this dimension.

"Never, ever wander off alone," he warns me. "You aren't old enough or strong enough, you don't have enough training to understand the dangers of these places" he says sternly.

He takes my hand, and we leave. I never again wander off alone, since I have experienced the unpleasant side of this dimension myself.

Later, when I am much older, I realized that Mattheo had allowed me to wander off, in order to teach me this important lesson while he was still close enough to protect me. I wandered through the first dimension during visits that occurred over the space of a year, riding on a beautiful silver pony with white ethereal wings and a long blue mane and tail, that would do my bidding if I fed it a bit of blood from a sacrifice I had done during the day.

I learned that the rulers on each dimension required a sacrifice in order to enter and leave safely. I was taught to always bring a "gift" (part of a sacrifice) when traveling. The first few visits, Mattheo had prepared my gift for me, but he expected me to bring my own "entrance and exit fees" by the fifth visit. At the young age of three, the gifts required of me, such as blood from a self-flagellation performed prior to travel, or bringing bits of a heart from an animal sacrifice, were lighter than those that would be required as I got older. I was not fully aware at this age just how dangerous travel, especially to be more advanced dimensions, would be.

When traveling, my spirit would leave my physical body, which appeared pale, cold and almost waxy, or even near death, in the room in the facility where it remained while I traveled. When I was a few years older, I would learn to monitor the bodies of those who were traveling, and to provide physical or emotional support if the traveler seemed in trouble. When I was older, I could only travel to a higher dimension, such as the 12th or 13th dimensions, by allowing my body to be subjected to extreme torture that would bring me to a near-death state. But this would be in the future. Now, I was still young, and unaware that this would be required one day.

Power battles

In the fourth dimension, there were structures that looked like large ziggurats. To go up the steps, a sacrifice had to be left on each step, or the way up would be blocked. I first went to this dimension at age seven with Mattheo.

I am seven years old. Mattheo is standing next to me on top of one of the ziggurats. As I look around in wonder, I see that there are ascended masters or their students in training, who are each standing on the top of a ziggurat. Suddenly, a bright blue light flashes out from the hands of one of the men who is in a dark blue robe. He is facing another man dressed in a dark robe with stars on it. The man he is facing also emanates a bright blue light, and the two battle for a time, until the one with stars on his robe finally concedes to the first man.

I am seeing my first power battle, one method of training that the ascended masters use to strengthen their power and to learn to withstand the pain of gaining power. It is a contest of spiritual strength and will between various masters, and also between their mentees, who also practice against one another.

"You will learn to do this soon," Mattheo tells me. "But remember to only battle those at your level; if you should irritate a higher master, they could kill you."

Mattheo lets me practice sending light out. My light is red (the lowest, weakest color). What surprises me is how much this hurts: it is incredibly, agonizingly painful to create this light.

I see another young apprentice who looks older than me, but his light is also red. I turn my light towards him, and he battles me, with an arrogant sneer on his face. But the expression on his face soon changes. I have a very strong theta ability for someone my age and am able to overcome the pain and wear him down, and win the battle. I send a "thanks" to the young mentee who let me practice, but he turns away.

Elated, I return from the dimension, back to the room in the facility, with Mattheo. After we rest a bit, and have something to eat and drink, he talks to me with a serious look on his face.

"Do not let this victory make you arrogant," he cautions me. "There are many who are stronger than you. It is best to watch and learn at first, and to appear much weaker than you actually are. Try not to show your full strength, or you will attract the attention of those much older and more dangerous than the young apprentice you sparred with today."

Through much practice over many years, at first with supervision, and eventually alone, I became able to emanate white-blue light from my hands. I became one of the stronger masters on this dimension, where I also took my own mentees. But I never battled the weak, or took advantage of those just learning, as some did. I never laughed at the wounds that some suffered while learning, because I knew how difficult – and dangerous – this all was.

Shape Shifting

I am nearly six years old and am in a stone cottage in the midst of woods with one of my spiritual mentors, Joan, another Jesuit father whose job is to teach me certain branches of mage craft.

For instance, when I was three years old, Joan gave me a white rabbit to take care of. Each day for two weeks, I brought it fresh greens and carrots, changed its water, and was allowed to play with the rabbit during free time.

At the end of two weeks, Joan came to me and said, "I want you to kill the rabbit." I was horrified. I had bonded to this little animal friend during the time I was there. I had talked to it, held it, and felt comforted by its soft fur and wiggling nose, a kind contrast to the strict, rigid requirements of learning spells correctly. I began sobbing and clutched the rabbit to my chest.

"No, no, no!" I screamed.

Joan took up a knife, took the rabbit and me over to a table. She put the knife in my hand and guided my hands as we killed it together. I was crying the whole time.

"You have to learn to give up the things you love; this is the greatest sacrifice for the most important spells," she told me.

I bit her; I was furious at what she had made me do.

Joan then took me over to a corner of the cottage where there was a dark, small area, possibly from an old oven. She put me in there and closed the door of bricks over it. She left me in the dark hole for 12 hours. I was shaken since I had thought she was going to leave me there forever, to die. The light in the room, even though it was evening, seemed too bright after being in the dark for so long.

While I blinked painfully, she told me, "You must never disobey me again like that, or I won't take you out." I never disobeyed her again.

I am six and a half years old. Joan and I have completed numerous incantations. I have gone into the woods and gathered herbs needed for various recipes, including for potent poisons as well as those used in some ancient rituals. By now, I know the herbs and roots by sight, and can gather them fairly quickly. I enjoy spending time in the woods, where the sunlight filters down, and the fresh smell of cedar and other trees is carried on the breeze.

Upon my return, Joan (who I think of privately as the "old crone" even though she is a top mage in the Order) tells me, "Today you will learn something that is more difficult than anything else you have done yet."

Then, as I watch, she turns into a bird – a large raven – in front of me, and flies into a nearby tree. She then flies back and turns back into her human shape. I have seen things like this before, but I am still surprised and a little afraid when she tells me, "Today, you will learn to change shape." I feel a bit wary.

Joan continues, "Changing shape is very, very painful, and I will only ask you to do so for a very short time at first. Part of your training to endure pain has been to help prepare you for doing this." She, and all of the fathers, always try to explain what will happen before teaching us to do new things. Even so, I feel afraid. I don't like pain, and I realize that yet another painful lesson is coming.

Together, we gather the sacrifices needed for this incantation to work. In addition to catching numerous live ravens over the past two weeks, which Joan has kept in cages outside the cottage, we also have live humans of various ages in cages. Shape shifting requires strong mage craft, and together we do the numerous sacrifices. We kill ravens, then position the humans to be sacrificed on a diagram of a raven, spreading their arms out like wings and arranging feathers from the ravens we killed on their arms and bodies. Then, on her command, I kill the humans.

Once the correct number of sacrifices are done, Joan then places feathers and blood on me, and has me recite the words of the ancient ritual, in the ancient original language of Babylon. I do so, and then feel excruciating, almost unbearable pain. I cry out from the pain, but my cry sounds like a loud "caw!" even though I still look human.

But then, slowly, feathers begin appearing, I grow smaller, and eventually I look like a small raven. My transformation has taken much longer than Joan's, but she says, "It is normal for the change to be slow at first. It will get faster and easier in the future".

The blinding pain distracts me, but Joan speaks again with a commanding voice. "Fly to the roof of the house behind us, sit there for 30 seconds, then fly back to me."

I do so, in sheer wonderment at what it feels like to fly upwards, perch on a roof, and then fly quickly down to the ground. I return, panting and almost passing out from pain at this point. Joan tells me, "Think the words of the incantation to return to human shape, while also trying to speak them. Don't worry if you sound like a raven at first, that will change."

I think and try to speak the ritual, terrified that I will be remain trapped in the painful shape forever, pain that feels as if it is killing me. My first words are weak "caws". But as I continue, gradually the feathers disappear, skin appears, and I can finish the ritual with words. I am fully human again, much to my relief, and the pain is nearly gone. Joan then has me make a sacrifice of thanks for the gift of the change and the return.

Afterwards she praises me. "It is very difficult and painful to change like this," she says. "It is a sign of your ability and discipline in learning mage craft that you can do this at your age. You are doing well, indeed."

I am glad that she is pleased but I also feel exhausted. I feel completely drained, as if I have climbed a high mountain. We go inside the cottage then, eat a light meal, and she lets me go to sleep early. The next morning, I return to the facility with Joan. "You will practice changing shape every five days, for increasing lengths of time," she says. "I will be with you while you learn."

Joan is true to her word. Once or twice each week, she takes me into the woods outside the facility, where I do the sacrifices and practice with her until I can change more quickly and keep a raven shape for a half hour at a time. This ability takes over a year to achieve.

As I grow older, Joan and other mage mentors teach me how to change into other animals: a wolf (the symbol of the Order – I change into a tawny and silver-haired wolf); and eventually, a dragon. These changes are always extremely painful, which limits how long I, or any of the other fathers, can maintain them.

I learn about tribes of people with a generational history of changing into wolves. They begin their own training extremely young and by the time they are adults, these wolf-people can maintain their shape for a full day. Nonetheless, it is painful for them, and if they try to maintain the change too long, they can become ill or even die. These tribes teach their members how to tell when they must turn back into human form.

As part of my mage training, when I am a teenager, I have to visit one of these tribes in a part of eastern Europe, live with them a week, and run in a wolf shape with them on several hunts. However, I can only maintain the wolf shape for a few hours, unlike them. I feel wary and cautious with these people. I never really trust them, but also understand that there is an ongoing relationship between our Order and theirs. This group was the one who originally taught the fathers the rituals needed to change into a wolf shape. I was taught that this was because at one time, several hundred years ago, one of the Jesuit fathers saved the life of one of their leaders, and in gratitude, he taught this skill to the father who saved him in return for the father sharing one of our secrets with him. Whether this is true, or legend, I don't know. But I did experience learning to change shape while training to become an ascended master.

When I was older, as a teen, I even enjoyed going out in a "pack" with other fathers, young and old, in wolf form. Mattheo was a beautiful silver and white wolf, while other fathers were wolves of varying size, colors and shape. The wolf was a favored shape because the wolf was considered the symbol of the Order, since we were taught that Romulus and Remus were the true founders of Rome and of the pagan rituals that the Order grew from.

Chapter 8: Learning to Become an Agent

Children in the Order are required become accomplished assassins and well-rounded agents. Our training to use every type of weapon skillfully, to kill others secretly and quietly, or even openly and violently, including in pogrom style as I grew older, was practiced frequently.

First Mission

I am three and a half years old and am an adorable waif with curly brown hair and huge, somewhat sad and wistful brown eyes. I am simply dressed in a white cotton dress with a red sash belt. My cheeks and lips have been lightly and expertly rouged by a father. I enter a lounge where soft piano music is playing and wait on a chair nearby.

After a time, the professional piano player takes a break. Another man sitting nearby goes to the piano and begins playing. He has brown hair and has been drinking a bit; he looks middle aged. As he plays, I go towards the piano, acting fascinated by the music and the man playing, as I have been taught to do. He looks up, sees me and smiles. I bat my eyes at him and listen for a time. Finally, I lisp, "I don't have a daddy. Will you be my daddy tonight?" This is a well-known code phrase used by children who are being trafficked in this wealthy part of Germany when they offer their services.

The man keeps playing but nods his head, so I know to wait. After a while, the regular piano player returns to the lounge. The man walks towards me, takes my hand, and we go to his room together. While he is undressing, I quickly put some powder from a packet into his drink while his back is turned. This powder has no taste but is a strong sedative. The man is keeping up a conversation with me in German and I give him short, childish responses. I have been carefully prepped for weeks regarding exactly what to say and not say to this man, and have practiced over and over before coming here.

As he sips his drink, he becomes sleepier. Finally, he draws me onto the bed with him and he attempts anal sex. But the sedative has taken effect, and he quickly falls asleep into a deep sleep. I then take a small white pin out of the pocket of my dress and carefully stab him in the heart with a potent, undetectable poison, as I have been taught. I wait and the man stops breathing. His body turns cold and pale.

I put my dress and other items into a small bag and retrieve a small outfit from the balcony that was placed there previously by an adult. I change into this outfit. I then walk down the hall and knock on the door of one of the rooms. A man I call "Uncle Lou" sees me, lets me in the room, and then goes into the room I was in previously to ensure that the man is dead.

"Aunt Sarah" then puts a blond wig on my head and wipes all the makeup off my face. She colors my eyebrows a lighter color and puts a prosthesis into my teeth to change the shape of my face slightly. I have already practiced all of these things over and over. "Aunt Sarah" then takes my hand. "Uncle Lou" meets us in the hall, and we all go together, a French family on vacation returning home by train. We go to the train station, the adults chatting and laughing in French, and I am a well-behaved little French girl.

Once in France, I am taken to a safe house, where Father Mattheo debriefs me on what has been my first mission. He holds me, tells me what a good girl I am, and says how proud he is of me. I feel conflicting feelings: glad that he is glad, but also, deep inside, sad and ashamed of what I have done. These feelings are buried deep inside though, and when he asks, "Are you okay?" I respond "Yes, I'm fine."

And I am. After all, the event I want to forget, as is now easy to do, is over; the event I want to remember, being held and loved and praised, is now happening, so things do seem fine. I have learned to completely separate my feelings about doing things that I really did not want to do from the things that I did like, and will continue to do so for many, many years.

The next day, as a special treat, I am given the day off from regular training. Father Mattheo takes me out for ice cream and then we go to the beach, where I feed the gulls and enjoy the sunshine. These are the moments that I live for, and I try to forget the cost that they come at. The events of the day before are already locked away deep in a special part of my mind and cannot cloud the events of this sun-filled, joyful time with the father I love most.

When this memory first came, I wept for the little girl that I was: a child used by the adults around her to accomplish their goals. I have no idea of why this man was killed. I only did what the people who raised me, people I loved, told me I had to do. But it is terrible to think that by this age, the fathers and Mengele had already overcome the innate reluctance to kill another human being to the point that I could follow out their orders so obediently. I also had to struggle with guilt and shame. Was I just a little baby who killed, a "little killer" as Mengele so often called me? Was this what I truly was? How could I have done this so young, unless the things that the adults around me told me were true, as much as I hated what they said about me?

But then, as time went on and I processed these and other feelings, I realized that I was a little girl who was very, very controlled and abused by the adults around her. A little girl desperate for love, affection and approval, one who knew that the only way to win this love, and escape terrible punishment, was to obey the orders I was given. It makes me sad to realize that the adults around me, people who should have been loving me, playing normal games with me, reading me children's stories and not torturing me, were unable to do so.

I had no access to normal love and affection, and instead, had learned to seek the only thing that was offered: a conditional love, the only kind of love the adults around me could offer. They could only offer me conditional love because they themselves were terrified of breaking the rules. They also had undergone their own childhood programming that made them slaves to fear, and they had passed this fear down to me through their modeling complete obedience to the demonic, their own self-punishments if they ever failed to perform, and their inability to freely love even those closest to them.

MI6

There is a house in the UK known as "Colonel Green's House" that is run by part of MI6. While there is no official record of this house existing, and most employees of MI6 have no idea of its existence, I was told that it was founded to train children in the arts of spy craft and assassination. According to my memories, the Jesuit Order and several others groups utilize this training facility run by 'six' (what we call MI6) and several of their trainers. My classes and other classes from the Order, several times over our childhood, attended training at this house.

I am three years old and am standing against a wall with the other children my age. A trainer I do not know is talking. "Here, you do not have names; you are numbers. I expect you to respond immediately when I call your number." She pins numbers on each of us. I am

"38", and for the rest of my time there and subsequent times, I will no longer be "Lucia" but simply "38". The boy next to me is "39". I wonder why we can't use our names but know that I will be scolded if I ask, since this trainer doesn't seem to like questions, only unthinking obedience. I contrast this with the fathers who welcome questions as long as they are intelligent ones, and who invite debate as part of learning. This trainer at six reminds me more of Mengele whose rule at times was "obey, don't talk".

I am outside, dressed in trousers and a sweater. There are woods nearby, and my job is to track the adult who has gone into the woods and find him, as quickly as possible. I run – I am fast for my age – and follow the trail of bent grasses into the woods. I have figured out where the adult went in, but now what? As I have been taught, I look at the ground for broken twigs, for disturbed leaves, at branches for any bent or moving twigs. I think I know which way the "hare" has gone, and as a "hound" I move through the woods.

Suddenly, I come to a stream and am unsure. I look on both sides of the stream. At that moment, a bird flies out of a tree. I look up, and there in the branches is the adult. When I see him, he smiles and says, "Very good!" He holds my hand and gives me a treat, as we go back to the training center.

When I am a bit older, I learn to trail others without being seen myself, or noticed, and how to blend into any scene in a way that I become almost invisible. I learn that this is called "tailing" someone, that I am "following a tag". When I am older still, I find it a challenge, but also fun, to learn to "drop a tail" and escape from the person pursuing me. This is like playing tag, but is much, much more serious. If I fail to find someone within an allotted time, I could be severely punished or reprimanded; I have seen this happen to other children. So far, I have always found the person in the time given.

I am at a rifle range. I am four years old, back for two weeks of training at six. Like the other children around me who are also practicing with guns, I can almost always hit the bull's-eye, and the trainer praises me as she walks by. I like shooting; it's fun and I am good at it. I like the challenge of trying to hit a target that is further and further away. I aim at the cutout figures of people and can almost always hit the head or heart dead on center. Dead, indeed; this is the whole goal of my training although I often do not think of this as I practice marksmanship with guns and rifles of varying types. I know that when I am six years old, I will be given my own permanent rifle and be allowed to name it. As an older child, I called my favorite rifle "Betsy", and she never let me down. She seemed to become a part of me at times as I went on various missions.

As a teen, "Becca", a longer, newer sniper rifle became my constant companion on missions where I needed to be able to make the long shot. I would pat her and say "Good girl" when a shot was successful at a long distance.

At six, my delta programming (a complex computer system for memory storage and retrieval) was also installed into my internal landscape over several years of intermittent visits there. They had a room with moving walls (that would threaten to crush any internal parts that remembered), and another room with a crystal ball that rotated, and flashing lights, that would punish and fracture parts (that had been given a psychedelic drug) for disobedience.

When these memories first came to me, I wondered why on earth the Jesuit fathers, who are accomplished in all of these skills themselves, bothered to take us to Green House for training. But later I remembered that for certain assignments, the people paying require that the agent be a certified six graduate and they wanted to see the documentation. So, the children are taught over several years, and gain their documentation that will allow them to take on these types of missions – and earn money for the Order.

Learning to Take on a Pack of Dogs

Part of my training was dealing with aggressive security dogs.

I am four years old. I am standing in an enclosed yard. It is a sunny, warm day, but I am anxious because of what is about to happen.

Suddenly, at the other side of the enclosed yard, a metal gate rises. An attack-trained dog comes snarling at me through the gate, running at full speed. When the dog gets to me, it lunges for my throat. I anticipate this, since I have learned how dogs attack, so I am ready in a crouch. I grab the dog by the neck with both hands, flip it on to the ground, place one foot on its right back leg to pin it to the ground, and twist its neck to break it. I get bitten as I twist, but that doesn't bother me; a bite is better than being killed.

I am shaking due to adrenaline. I know that if I had hesitated or made a mistake, I could have been badly hurt.

Father Mattheo and Father Carlotti both come over to me; they have been carefully watching this exercise to see how I do, and also to intervene if a mishap occurs.

"You did very well," Mattheo tells me.

"You were quick and sure," Carlotti enthuses, beaming proudly.

"Let me look at your bite," Mattheo says. The bite is not deep, and both fathers walk me to the medical treatment room. There, the wound is quickly healed with state-of-the art technology. The wound closes, with no scarring in the layers of the muscle or skin.

Afterwards, I go with the fathers to have a cup of coffee with lots of cream and a bit of sugar added.

"I liked how quick your reaction time was when you flipped the dog," Mattheo tells me. "I am very happy with how you did. But you grabbed the dog a little too low – that's why you got bitten. Next time, grab it higher up; it will be less likely to get a bite in if you do that."

"I agree," Carlotti says. "You did very well overall, but you just grabbed the dog a little too low and exposed your arm. Think about keeping your arm out of the way next time."

The fathers always combine praise with suggestions for improvement. Also, when a new skill is executed sufficiently well, there is always a reward, such as coffee. The greatest reward is not the coffee, though. It is the extra time I get to spend with two of the fathers I love most. I get to talk with them not just about the training exercise, but after reviewing the exercise, about other topics, for a full extra half hour that day.

As I get older, this exercise becomes much harder.

I am nine years old. The fathers have released a pack of four dogs at one time into the enclosure. These are full-grown Rottweilers, and much larger than those I had to kill when I was younger. I immediately take down the leader of the pack, as I have been taught. As I am now larger and stronger, I no longer need to try to pin the dog on the ground to be able to break its neck; I twist its neck while it is still in the air, and throw its body at the second dog (the dog next in the pack hierarchy to the alpha) which I had identified as soon as they had come through the gate. This makes the dogs pause for a moment. I grab and flip the second dog, breaking its neck at the same time, then again, I throw its body at the third dog. At this point, the third and fourth dogs look wary. I approach the third dog which is growling with its hackles up. Unhesitant and expertly, I grab it behind the ears, then twist its neck and throw the body at the remaining dog, which backs away from me and growls. Finally, I kill the last dog.

Afterwards, Father Carlotti and Father Timothy enter the enclosure and walk towards me.

"Very good, very good indeed," says Carlotti.

"You have learned very well," Timothy says. "I think you have earned a nice lunch."

The fathers help me lift the bodies of the dead dogs and place them in a special container for disposal. We walk into the facility, change into civilian clothes, and meet at a tunnel beneath the facility where a dark blue car is parked. Soon, we are all seated at a patio table outside a trattoria nearby to have a nice lunch. This is how they show their pleasure in me; they are beginning to treat me more as a peer and less like a small child in these small ways. To an outsider, of course, and I look like a young child going out for a meal with a parent and relative. As always, I treasure this special time given to me as a reward for doing well during an exercise.

Learning to kill dogs trained for military or security use is commonly a basic part of training for children in many occult societies and government agencies, including the Jesuit Order. I describe the training here in barehanded methods, but I was also taught to use many other methods, such as knives and poisoned bait. In the Order, when the children first start practicing barehanded kills of real dogs, to keep things within the child's physical capacity, small but aggressive dogs are used. These are typically puppies around 10 months old from breeds known for aggression and strong bites, such as German Shepherds, Dobermans and so on, who have been trained to lunge at and attack any child in that enclosure. While these dogs are small, to the four-year-old who believes that the dog will tear her apart if she makes a mistake, the dog does indeed seem the size of a massively huge dog.

The Fathers always pair achievements with reward. For the rest of my life, I will associate sitting and having a cup of coffee, and simply chatting, with love and reward, a sense of being valued and of a job well done. When I am much, much older, after a busy day in the programming labs, I will look forward to having a quick cup of coffee with my twin sister or brother, or with an older, beloved student that I am mentoring.

Sex Parties

I am four years old. My twin sister, Elizabeth, and I are naked, covered only with dark blue velvet cloaks. Around our necks are jeweled collars, and we are being led in on a lease as if we are a pair of dogs by one of the fathers. Once inside the huge room which is filled with adults in various states of dress and undress, many with wine or cocktail glasses in the hand, we wait.

There is a large raised pedestal in the middle of the room. It is about four feet by four feet, made of granite, with small steps in the back. Liz and I watch as one by one, young children are led up to the pedestal. They must stand, naked, while adults in the room "bid" for the chance to have sexual activities with each child for the night. The trainers discuss the sexual training that each child has, and bids are made with small, hand-held fans encrusted with jewels, scarlet and blue patterns, and gold leaf. Winners of each bid come up to the platform to collect their prize for the night.

Liz and I are two of the lucky ones. We each have a special temporary tattoo that lets those bidding know that we cannot be killed, although we can be used for anything else. This tattoo is a reminder that if we are killed, the person who killed us will suffer severe consequences, due to our "belonging" to an extremely influential person who wants us kept alive. We are on "loan" for the night, supposedly by the German father over the Illuminati, and we are supposedly his bastard children who have other skills that make him want us alive.

At some point, Liz and I are taken and led by our leashes onto the pedestal. I feel ashamed and embarrassed to be on display, naked, before a roomful of people, but have learned to hide this. I smile and look excited and coquettish at this "privilege". An individual can bid for one, or both of us. This night, two separate people bid for us. The one who bids and wins me is an older woman who is dressed only in a necklace, bracelets and earrings made of diamonds. The diamonds sparkle in the dim lights as I go to her. She does not tell me her name, but it is obvious that she is wealthy and powerful, not only from her jewels, but her body language and speech.

"What can you do, little girl?" she asks. While the trainer has already discussed my skills, she wants to hear it from me; maybe this is some type of test, or maybe she wants to humiliate me further.

"What do you like?" I reply, as I have been coached by my trainers.

She smiles and describes her favorite extremely sadistic activities. Her teeth are white and gleaming as she smiles. With dismay, I realize that those same teeth will be used soon to bite me in extremely sensitive, private areas. I tremble slightly, knowing that this is what she wants to see, but my reaction is not completely acting. I am sorry a woman bid because they can be some of the cruelest, most sadistic abusers. It is almost as if they have spent years devising ways to give "payback" for their own early sexual abuse but with interest. I have always wondered why they seem to be most vicious to little girls, wondered whether this is working out their own childhood abuse on a child that reminds them of themselves, but I never voice this out loud to a client. I do voice these thoughts with the fathers during debriefing afterwards.

I perform well. I let the sadistic woman have her way with me for hours. She seems very inventive, and I feel worn out emotionally and physically by the early morning. I am also sore everywhere. I have screamed appropriately, sensing that this is what this woman wants to hear as she abuses me. Finally, finally she herself is tired and falls asleep. Quietly, I get up and look for my twin. I worry about her in situations like this, as I know she worries about me. Tattoo or no tattoo, there is always the concern that a client might get carried away and go too far; many enjoy abusing children to death. But to my great relief, I see her sitting in a corner of the room, half asleep.

The father who brought us in, who is thought of in the German Illuminati as one of their trainers, but is actually a Jesuit father, sees that we are done with our clients. He brings my sister and me our cloaks. We are grateful to be covered, that the night is almost over, and leave with him. Outside, he takes us into a waiting van, unsnaps our leashes, and talks to my sister and me.

"You did very well," Father Carlotti starts. "You both performed perfectly with the clients."

I then realize that like me, he also had concerns, and was monitoring both of us and our clients closely during the night in hopes to intervene in time if something life-threatening seemed to be imminent.

Carlotti asks, "What did you learn while you were there?" He is asking us for intel, prompting us to report the conversations among adults in the room that we were listening to throughout the night, adults who did not suspect that four-year-old children were capable of being agents with photographic memories who would report any information discussed by them while in a drunken state. We give him the information he requests.

Once we are in a safe house not too far away, one owned by the Order, Lizzie and I are given baths, and wash off the body fluids that our clients left with us. We are also given medications to help prevent disease. Father Carlotti inspects us carefully to ensure that there is no significant harm. He provides healing technology for a rectal laceration that I have, and a gash in my twin's arm inflicted by her client, a male, biting her.

"Human bites are the worst," he mutters, as he cleans out the bite with a special formula, applying healing so that no scar is left. He then says to both of us, "I am so proud of you. I love you so much."

Lizzie and I then go to sleep in soft, warm beds that are side-by-side. I go to sleep holding my sister's hand.

"I love you, Lizzie" I tell her.

"I love you, Luce", she answers, and then we sleep for hours. There will be no training routine tomorrow; we are given a day off to spend with each other and one of the fathers. They understand how difficult nights like the previous one can be on very young children and give us this small respite. Of course, the day after our rest, we go back to our normal routine.

Of course, Lizzie and I told ourselves that we were two of the "lucky ones" with the special tattoo. We had seen and heard far too many children who were called expendable by the adults around us die slow, terrible deaths at these parties. Secretly, deep inside, however, I wonder if the children who died, who no longer have to experience any more pain, were the lucky ones. I can't say this to Lizzie, or she will be forced to let the fathers know, and this will be emotionally painful for her. So I keep silent.

All children in the Jesuit Order are trafficked, but we did not define it that way. Attending and being abused at these types of parties held by the extremely wealthy in Europe and other countries was framed as doing a "mission", one that involved a specific set of skills, skills that could "help the Order." What we did was not defined as being abused, but as participating in a potentially dangerous activity. But all missions were dangerous to some extent. We were allowed to be "real agents" according to the fathers, and they were using our deep desire to do great things for the Order, when we were put in these situations.

But the reality is that my twin sister and I, and all of the other children I grew up with, were being terribly sexually abused and trafficked. The fathers who forced us to do this had been subjected to non-stop sexual abuse as children themselves. They did not realize how monstrous what they were asking us to do was; after all, they had to do it when they were young as well.

But the terror, anguish, sadness, grief and sense of betrayal, along with deep rage at the father who led my sister and me into this potentially life-threatening situation, risking our lives for the sake of gaining useful information, came forward as I processed this memory.

Early Testing

Starting at a very young age, I learned how to do various missions, practicing extensively within first the facility, and later on the streets of Rome. Even as a toddler, I would be taken into a room where there were various adults talking. Later, I would be asked by a father questions such as "How many people were in the room?" "How were they dressed?" "Who had the nicest clothes?" "Who spoke the most?" This was very early training for debriefing after a mission, when I would be required to remember even the most minute details and share them concisely and clearly with the person I was to report to after a mission.

I also had to practice completely forgetting a mission after it was over, in order to maintain a high level of security around these missions, as needed. Parts who had memories of the mission had to give their memories to our security storage system within delta system which enabled them to completely forget that an event had occurred. We were not required to forget all missions, but had to be able to do so for particular missions when ordered to.

I am three years old. I have just seen an adult stabbed in front of me by Father Mattheo. Afterwards, I help him put the body into a bag and clean up the room, wiping it down quickly and carefully with a special solution that destroys blood cells or body fluids. We are dressed in special gear, with nets over our hair, gloves, disposable booties and aprons. Looking like fugitives from an operating room in our gear, we completely clean the room, put the body on a trolley and wheel it into a cold room for later dissection by one of the classes.

We then take our protective clothing off, dispose of it in a trash bag, and place the bag into a chute that goes to an incinerator. Mattheo takes me into a white room next door. He gives an amnesia code, awaits, then asks, "Do you remember what happened in the other room?"

He looks intently at me, and I tremble. I remember seeing Mattheo kill the man, and our cleaning. The memory is fuzzy, but still there.

"I...I...I don't know," I say, hesitating to answer because I don't want to anger Mattheo.

"What don't you know?" he asks in a stern but quiet tone. I realize he is angry. Mattheo does not put up with equivocating, and I realize to my dismay that I must tell the truth.

"I remember some," I say.

"Tell me exactly what you remember," he responds. This is an order, and I must obey.

So, I tell him about seeing him stab the man, and our cleaning up afterwards.

"Don't you know that you MUST forget?" Mattheo says. His tone is urgent. He then takes a gun out and points it at my temple. "If you don't learn to forget, I will have to shoot you. I can't let you be a security risk, no matter how much I love you. Now, forget!"

He gives the command. I sweat and try my best to give the memory away to Secundus, one of my main delta controllers, for memory storage. If I don't succeed, I will die, I know it. I have heard that Mattheo shot another child in a previous class who could not learn to forget on command by a certain age – that child was never seen again - and I am at that age.

"Do you remember what happened in the other room a few minutes ago?" Mattheo asks me. I blink and look at him, bewildered. What other room? What is he talking about?

I am wearing special equipment to monitor my physical responses and brain activity. "What room?" I ask. Mattheo looks at the monitors and smiles, looking relieved.

"What is the last thing you remember?" he asks me.

"I remember going for ice cream with you last weekend," I tell him. He smiles again, and says, "Today, I will take you out for ice cream again." He takes the equipment off, and as he promised, I get to enjoy some delicious gelato, one of my favorite treats, with him, the father I love most. I have no idea that he has just threatened my life an hour before and I enjoy the warm sunshine and the soft breeze as we walk down the street during a beautiful Rome spring day.

I am four years old. I have been told to go into a room to stab an adult who is sitting tied to a chair (a homeless man who was used for this training) in the heart, and then to go to a sink, wash the knife off, change my clothes, and go into another room and sit down.

I obey my instructions perfectly. I stab the adult, who screams in terror when seeing a knife-wielding child come near him and also during the stabbing. Blood trickles from the knife wound. Carefully, I carry the knife to a sink in the corner of the room, wash it with antiseptic soap, and then place the knife into a small carrier. I pick the carrier up, walk out of the room, and enter another room through a door. I place the carrier on a white table in the center of the room, then sit in a white chair. The room is completely white: white walls, white floors, white windows; all is white here, the color of amnesia, forgetfulness and comfort. I hear a command given to forget what has just occurred on a large monitor screen inside the room, along with several visual codes that reinforce this command. The codes to bring out Lucia, my cult host, are then given in the same way.

Father Carlotti, one of the fathers I love, comes into the room. "Lucia, how are you?" he asks.

"Fine," I answer. I am fine, since as Lucia, my cult host, I have already forgotten what has just happened. I was not "out" for the actual stabbing, and so have no memory of what had just occurred. Looking intently at my face and eyes, Carlotti nods. He can tell by my body language, posture, speech, pupils and breathing that yes, I truly don't remember.

"Can I speak with Axle?" he asks. Axle, the part in me that did the stabbing, comes out. Axle likes to stab with knives and axes and has learned the art of killing using many different weapons. Carlotti places special monitoring equipment on my chest and head.

"Axle, what just happened in the other room?" Carlotti asks.

"What other room?" Axle asks. Like Lucia, he has no memory of the previous event; his memory has already been sent to delta system. Carlotti checks the monitoring equipment and nods. The brainwave activity indicates no response to the question other than would be normal; if the trauma was remembered, there would be a sharp spike in several physical and other parameters, including increased brainwave activity in certain areas of the brain.

"Do you remember anything happening today?" Carlotti continues assessing for amnesia, or its lack.

"I went to lunch, but that was a week ago," Axle responds, referring to a reward lunch of his favorite foods at a local trattoria with Father Jerome. "Why are you asking?" Axle looks slightly bewildered and suspicious but has no idea of why he is being interrogated. He has passed the test. Carlotti takes the equipment off, and takes Axle out for lunch again, since he has performed well and forgotten the things he is supposed to.

Axle and other parts have learned by age four to completely forget. Numerous scenarios, carefully designed by the fathers, have taught them how important amnesia is not just to security and protecting the fathers who they loved, but for survival itself.

Maintaining complete amnesia for missions is critical for maintaining security and secrecy for this occultic organization involved in criminal activities. The fathers bond closely to the children they love, but they cannot allow any child that cannot forget when told to, to live. I felt heartbroken when the memory of Mattheo threatening my life came, because I felt my own terror as a child that I would die and also heartbreak that this father I loved so much was capable of killing me if I could not perform this task. I loved HIM, why couldn't he love me the same way? This is how I felt, thinking I would never threaten Mattheo's life, no matter what. The heartbreak came from realizing that while the love seemed real, it was limited by the demands of keeping the security of the organization, and of keeping the demonic beings that the fathers worshipped happy. To my great and growing grief, I realized that what I had labeled "love" as a child was indeed love, but only to a limited extent, held within certain parameters. And that my own ability to love would be used against me, without hesitation.

Chapter 9: A Walk in the Garden

I loved the times alone that I could spend with the fathers I loved, especially Mattheo. During these times, I could ask him the questions that I had and he always gave me wise counsel, or at least understanding. This was a critical part of my training to become a father and mentor myself one day.

It is a beautiful sunny day. I am sitting on a stone bench near the wall that surrounds the monastery where I go to school. Climbing roses go up a trellis behind us, their perfume filling the air. It is springtime in Italy, and I am sitting on the bench next to Mattheo. He is in his black robe, and I am in my little brown acolyte robe. I am eight years old, and our conversation is intense.

"If we love each other, why did I have to hurt my (twin) sister Lizzie last night?" I ask. I am heart-broken. The night before, I went into Satan's room at the Vatican, a dark room that the fathers would lead me into on certain nights, then leave me alone in it until morning.

Satan had appeared in his hideous, ugly form in front of me. "Do you love me?" he asks.

I hate that question, but I respond, "Of course I do."

"Then show me," he says. I shudder internally, but completely hide my reaction. I know that "showing love" will require doing something that I especially hate.

"Go and get Elizabeth, your sister, and bring her into this room," he says. The words echo in the room. I feel cold chills of terror, afraid that one of us will die this night.

I leave the room and see Mattheo. He looks surprised that I have left the room so quickly, but then he sees my pale face and the expression in my eyes. "What happened?" he asks.

"I have to bring Lizzie here and go into the room with her," I whisper.

Mattheo turns pale, probably wondering the same thing. "I will get her, wait here," he says. In a few minutes, he returns with a frightened Lizzie.

Shaking, I take her hand and we enter the room together, hand in hand.

"Who do you love more, me or her?" Satan demands of me, pointing at my twin.

I don't know how to respond. I have been taught all my life to love and obey Satan, but...I love Lizzie deeply. She and Dannie, my other twin, are the two human beings that I trust with some of my inmost thoughts. We play together, tease each other, and I can bounce ideas with Lizzie. She is bright and intelligent, and loves sciences like I do. She, too is showing special aptitude as a trainer. She and I compare notes and try to solve problems together when we are alone together. We sometimes cuddle up together at night, even though each of us has a narrow bed in our class dormitory. Lizzie is in another class, the second class, which sleeps in the next dorm room over, but she and Dannie sometimes sneak into my bed at night, or vice versa, for a cuddle and whispered conversation before we fall asleep. While this is technically breaking the rules, it is allowed at times, since the fathers realize the need for comfort especially after particularly demanding or stressful days.

"Stressed" does not begin to describe my feelings as Satan waits for my answer. If I lie, I completely believe that he will know.

"I love you both deeply" I reply, knowing that I have to give the honest answer. "I love you even more for allowing me to have a sister like Lizzie."

Lizzie and I tremble slightly and wait for what seems a long, long, time, both of us wondering if I will have to kill her tonight. It is not unusual for Satan to demand terrible sacrifices in these late-night meetings in this awful room which I have come to dread. I have been visiting Satan in this room since I was a very young child and know from the upset expression on Mattheo's face when he brings me here that he also does not like this room no matter how much he verbalizes the "honor" to me of being chosen to visit at such a young age.

Lizzie and I wait and wait. We have to look lovingly at Satan and no longer hold hands. Showing too much affection now would be disastrous with this jealous creature. Finally, Satan speaks. "I want you to peel the skin off of your sister's upper arms and legs and offer her screams to me as a sign of your affection. This will be a sacrifice from both of you," he says. I understand that I will be allowed to apply artificial skin to keep her alive as I do this. He is not asking for her death — at least not tonight.

Lizzie and I are both relieved; she can be healed from peeling if I use the artificial skin and take her into the healing room right afterwards. I take out small golden instruments from a dark blue velvet bag, a bag containing the instruments that the Torturer's Guild has been teaching me to use correctly the past few years. I know how to peel skin off without killing the victim and am careful to go slowly and carefully with my sister. She screams because she has been told to. She does not send the pain down to her pain holders, but instead, endures the pain herself in her cult host and other presenting parts. The sound is terrible and my hands shake a little as I perform this task, but I do my best to still them. I do not want to hurt her more than I have to. With each section, I cover her with artificial skin, one of the life-saving technologies that we have developed.

After several hours, I am done. Satan smiles. I take the skin and put it on a special altar in the room and move back. He then consumes the skin, smacking his lips grotesquely.

He turns to my almost unconscious sister. "Your sister's act of love has been most delicious to me," he tells her.

I am trying not to faint, as I know what he now requires. "Thank you for your gratitude, gracious lord," I say. "I enjoy giving you these services and feel honored to be your servant this night."

Finally, finally he leaves the room, disappearing in a flash. In spite of the artificial skin, Lizzie is shivering. I run and get Mattheo, and he gently carries Lizzie into the healing technology room, where her skin is regrown. There will be no physical scars, but the emotional scars and pain of this night will last a lifetime for both my sister and me.

The next day, while walking with Mattheo in the garden, I share with him my questions about the previous night.

"Why does Satan demand such terrible things?" I ask him. Because the night before was so difficult, I have been given a half day off from school, and Mattheo is spending extra time with me. Father Carlotti is spending extra time with Lizzie, who has also been given a half day off from school. I am crying as I ask this question, because with Mattheo, I can show how I truly feel about things like this. There are some things that even he does not allow me to question or show feelings about, but asking this type of question is part of my own training, and he is my primary mentor.

Mattheo pauses and looks sad. "Sometimes, there are things that are difficult to understand," he says. I wonder if he is remembering similar things required of him when he was younger. "The more promise a person shows, the more difficult the things that are asked of him or her," he says. I realize that this man, who is a top general in the Jesuit army, has had to face this kind of trauma in his own life. "As mortals, we cannot understand everything we are asked to do," he says.

"But it's cruel! It's wrong!" I cry out. "How can this be good, or part of immortality?!?"

I am deeply questioning my training, and am on the edge of going too far, but I can't help it. I feel guilty, ashamed, and heartbroken over what I was forced to do the night before. I know without being told that had I not given the sacrifice of pain demanded the night before that my sister would have been killed to punish me. But even knowing this, my mind, spirit and emotions are rebelling against the cruelty which I cannot reconcile with obedience to the beautiful beings and the belief in ascension towards immortality that I have been indoctrinated with.

Because Mattheo is wise, he listens to my pain and waits as I pour out to him how unfair it all is. He holds me in his arms as I cry and wail. Finally, when I am quiet, he continues. "I understand how painful this is," he says. There is something in his voice and his eyes that lets me realize that he has undergone similar traumas. "Those who show the most promise, are at times asked to give the most in return." He looks sad and holds me for a while. "We as mortals cannot always understand the ways of the immortals," he continues. "There are things that I still don't understand. But I have to believe – and you also need to believe – that the sacrifice last night was for your and Liz's good; to help you both give up a bit of your mortal, fleshly desires to help you ascend."

It is not his words, but his understanding and comfort that help me the most.

I watch the bees buzzing and pollinating the flowers behind our bench. Mattheo then rises, and picks a pink rosebud, and brings it to me. He takes a pin out of a pocket in his robe and pins it to my robe above my heart. "This is what you are to me, a beautiful flower, with sweet perfume for those who love you," he says tenderly.

We go to his private office, and have a cup of tea together and talk some more about everyday things. I then go to lunch, proudly wearing the rose. I will wear it until it begins to dry out, then carefully press it between the leaves of a book.

One day, when I am a father, my symbol will be a pink rose as a reminder that I am loved. Mattheo's symbol is a red rose; Jerome's is an off-white rose, and Carlotti's is a pale, creamy yellow rose. On certain special occasions, the fathers wear their special rose pinned to their robes, and I will do the same when I am older.

As this memory illustrates, the Jesuit fathers are completely deceived. They have developed a twisted logic that justifies the cruelty and abuse that the demonic demands. They actually believe that terrible things such as this are for a "greater good." When I first had this memory, I went through horror, shame, and guilt that I actually did this to my sister, and deep rage at the fathers and at Satan for perpetuating this type of horrific abuse on small children. Lizzie and I had no one to rescue us at this age. I tried to be my sister's rescuer by saving her life, as I had been taught to do for those I love. But I was a child, and I could not rescue her, or myself, or anyone else, from the terrible acts and the destructive, false beliefs that we were indoctrinated with through scenarios like this.

I also met parts inside who completely believed what the fathers had taught them: that pain is for a "greater good"; that all of this spiritual activity that caused such emotional, spiritual and physical wounding was worth it, and was helping us to overcome our mortality. They had completely accepted the beliefs modeled to them by their caregivers, the Jesuit fathers. It took a long time, and my overcoming my own horror at realizing that they believed in abuse that would bring ascension as much, or even more strongly than I believed in Christianity. On my healing journey, this brought on many quite heated discussions inside me.

Finally, an internal helper told me, "Shut up, stop preaching, and just listen to them. Otherwise, they will hate you, because you are proving to them that all Christians are self-righteous little prigs." This was the best advice anyone has ever given me. While uncomfortable at first, I started to shut up, stop preaching, and listen. I held hands inside, without judging, and memories began pouring out as I started to realize that their beliefs were my own beliefs; that deep down inside, without knowing it, I also had believed this same thing. It took time, questioning a lot, and learning to love these parts and forgiving myself, for the healing to proceed and for this and similar scenes to become a memory, and not an ongoing internal trauma.

Remember the Flowers

Not all walks in the gardens with the father brought comfort. It was an essential part of my early training for parts to "remember to forget" the memories that they have been ordered to forget. This section describes another one of the many memories I have about being trained to forget.

I am about five years old. It is a slightly cloudy day, but the sun through the clouds is still bright. I love the outdoors, and always check the weather each day in hopes that my classmates and the other classes can all play outside after lunch during our free time. I love running, playing tag, soccer, and other games.

However, today, I do not get to play as I usually do. Instead, Father Mattheo comes over to me after lunch, and takes me by the hand. "We are going on a special walk today," he says. I am eager because I love having special time alone with this father outside of our 15-minute daily talks at the end of the day. Since it is late spring, there will be green grass and lots of beautiful flowers to see and smell, and birds to watch, as we walk.

We walk together down a stone-paved pathway to one of the deep fountains that pours water from its center up to the sky. I have often enjoyed sitting on the brown stone wall with flat pavements on top that surrounds the fountain in a circle, watching the water splash up and then back into the small moat of water surrounding the fountain. Mattheo and I are talking about our days. I have no idea of what is about to happen. We come to the fountain, and I look into the water. To my horror, I see the fountain moat filled with bodies — dead bodies — and each has a flower in its mouth. The bodies look like people I know, but cold, waxy, slightly blue and lifeless, staring with sightless eyes towards the sky. They bob almost silently in the water. I start to shrink away, unable to bear the sight.

"Look!" Mattheo says sharply. "I want you to see this." I look. Some of the arms on the bodies bob slowly in the soft current created by the splashing water. It is creepy beyond belief. I desperately, desperately want to look away. One of the bodies, that of a man, has a slightly open mouth and terrified eyes, as though he died screaming from terror. I see blood oozing from his mouth, slowly staining the water near his mouth red-pink.

"These are people who remembered things that they shouldn't," Mattheo tells me. "This is their judgement for their sins, to die this way. Let them be a reminder to you to never remember things that you have been told to forget."

He takes me around the water, and on the other side, I see children, including a young girl my age who looks so much like me. Like the man, her dead eyes are wide open in terror. She evidently died in great terror. Due to her likeness to me, I feel a sense of dread and horror like a chill creep up my spine. In the middle of her screaming mouth is a peony blossom, its white creamy color and beauty incongruent with the horrifying scenario I am seeing.

"Even children are punished if they remember too much," Mattheo says. "Everyone is expendable, if they remember too much, or without authorization."

I understand authorization: I am only allowed to remember, even in my cult host, the things I have been authorized to remember by the fathers. I am now seeing the terrible end result of going outside of authorized memories. Mattheo stoops down and looks at me at eye level. "Remember the flowers," he tells me softly but with great authority. "Remember the flowers: what you have seen today, and never forget the flowers." He then hands me a creamy peony, just like the one in the little girl's mouth.

As he does so, the realization dawns that by flowers, he means the dead bodies floating in the water. Some look like fathers I love. This causes me to panic, wondering if they, too, have remembered too much on this terrible day. I return to the dining room, shaking. To my great relief, an hour later I see two of the fathers I love, fathers who resemble the dead bodies I saw in the water. They are alive.

I am shaken deeply by this experience. That night, I have screaming nightmares of dead bodies floating underwater, opening their mouths in silent screams. I wake up, sweating and shaking. Mary Beth, my third (I am first, or group leader; Conner is my second, and Mary Beth is third in rank in my class and along with Conner, is one of the children in my class I am closest to) hears my cries and climbs into bed with me. She holds me until I calm down then we both go back to sleep. She does not ask what I dreamed. I do not tell her, since we both know that our dreams are often based on traumatic experiences, of which there are all too many. I am grateful for my classmate who is closer than any sister. For the rest of my life, when I hear the phrase "remember the flowers" I will become completely amnesic to whatever I am asked to forget.

It is not until I am older, and a father myself, that I learn that the bodies in the water are actually realistic manikins, that can be used over and over again in various scenarios. Neither do I know that during this week, one by one children at a certain age go for "special walks" with the fathers they love to encounter this gruesome scene and to learn to "remember the flowers".

This and other kinds of amnesia training are done because once the children in the Order get older, they are often sent on high-security missions that could create a security risk for the Jesuits if the parts that did the mission remember what was done, or if they disclose during interrogation by enemies. The Jesuits often used our attachment to loved ones, such as in the memory above, in order to gain the amnesia – and resulting silence – that they wanted. Even the cult host, who generally remembers most of life, will be ordered at times to completely forget an event. This is one of many methods used to ensure amnesia, and thus maintaining secrecy.

Chapter 10: Learning to Become a Trainer

I am three years old. I am proudly walking behind the fathers as they begin doing their rounds in their white lab coats, where they will do the first of their twice-daily assessments on the infants. I am being allowed to watch and learn. Mattie, one of the female trainers who at the age of 15 is extremely skilled and already considered a top trainer, places me on a high stool that enables me to look into the crib where she is doing her assessment.

"You must be very quiet and not talk while I am doing the assessment, otherwise you might distract the baby and mess up the results," she cautions me.

I silently nod my little head. Mattie approaches the infant, named Barnabas, who is four months old. The infant smiles and holds up his arms to be held. "Good, good," Mattie murmurs. This child is socializing well, and just as importantly, has learned to dissociate his fear of the trainers who bring pain, from his joy at receiving positive attention from the same trainers. A part who only views Mattie as a loving caretaker is out and greets her eagerly.

Mattie does a quick but careful head to toe assessment of his physical condition, including neurological reflexes. She checks for any signs of stress, looking at his weight, which is automatically charted by computer daily on the electronic display at the end of Barnabas's crib. "You've been eating well," she coos at the baby. It is obvious watching Mattie that she really loves this baby, and is attached to him, just as she is to the other infants in the nursery. This is a crucial aspect of a good trainer that I am absorbing by watching her interact with Barnabas; Mattie really likes this baby, and the baby knows it.

After some play time, Mattie calls out other parts in Barnabas. Today, she will be checking if the programming is intact in several systems, including the newly created internal hell system, where internal controllers with names like "Abbadon" and "Shiva" have been created through extreme trauma. "Abbadon, code 3351, come out," Mattie says, while simultaneously pushing a button that displays a unique black and white pattern of black and white squares, diamonds and half diamonds above his crib. These patterns and others are unique to the Jesuit order. I have already learned that they are never to be shared with *outsiders* or *strangers*; people who are not part of our Order.

Abbadon comes forward. Immediately, smiling Barnabas turns into an angry, hissing baby. Abbadon must guard the gates to the internal hell and has been carefully trained come out only at the appropriate codes, and face and voice recognition of a primary trainer. Mattie places a small helmet-shaped device over Abbadon's head, which will run specially designed videos of hell that shows him the importance of guarding hell to prevent chaos in the universe. Afterwards, Mattie takes the helmet off. "What do you do if a stranger tries to enter hell?" Mattie asks. Abbadon kicks his little fists and feet in an intensely violent, angry reaction, showing his intent to destroy anyone who tries to do so. "Good Abbadon, good, you want to protect your people," Mattie says. She picks him up and cuddles him, telling him he is doing good.

She conducts similar assessments of other system controllers. I watch as she gently and carefully checks that the programming is intact. If it is intact, she plays a sequence of colored lights and tones, which indicate programming integrity for that system; the tones and lights will vary for each system controller. She then gives each controller, including Abbadon, a drop of sweet water on their tongues to reward them for doing well, telling each how 'good' they are.

Later, Mattie takes me to the staff room that the trainers use to take breaks in. She gets herself a large mug of black coffee from coffee machine. "What did you learn, Luce?" she asks me. "What surprised you the most, and what did not?" Mattie is a good trainer. She has worked with me for the past few years, and I love her.

"I was surprised to see how different Barnabas looked when you called Abbadon and some of the other immortals out," I say. "It was a little bit scary." I have been programmed myself but have not been present before to watch another child being programmed.

"You're right, it is a real change," she affirms. "But these changes are important; Barnabas by himself could not guard his system from outsiders," she says. "He needs help from beings like Abbadon to have the strength to do so." I have learned to fear and hate the evil *outsiders* and *strangers*, people whose greatest desire in life seems to be to destroy the beloved Order and those within it. I have met these *strangers* and *outsiders* in carefully planned setups and know that they like to rape and hurt little children and laugh when the children are terrified or cry out in pain. I know how important it is to protect systems from *outsiders* and see the logic of her argument based on these experiences. But my stomach still felt funny seeing a tiny face turn so quickly from smiles to rage and violence, and I hope that when I am working with someone who has this part programmed into them, that he would not turn on me.

"Could he hurt you when he gets bigger?" I ask. Mattie smiles because the trainers encourage questions from their young protégées and she is glad that I am verbalizing this fear to her. This is why I am with her today: to watch, learn and have my questions answered.

"It would be possible, except he knows that I love him, and want to help him protect his systems, too," Mattie explains. She explains how important having a loving bond is when working with babies and children who have powerful internal protectors. "Unless he feels threatened by me or thinks I will hurt him or his parts unreasonably, he won't try to hurt me," she says. She then explains that he will be given appropriate targets for his rage as he gets older. I assume that she means *strangers*, not understanding at this young age that she actually means sending his rage into internal self-punishment and internal programming systems which torture internal parts for any independent thought or disobedience to the Order. I am still too young to be initiated into the "divide and conquer" mentality, in which trainers teach systems to turn on one another, and direct their rage to objects than those who are actually abusing them. Today, we are sticking to the basics, and it will be several years before I learn these other things.

I cannot wait to be a trainer like Mattie and the other fathers. I look up to them so much, these people who hold me, feed me, love me, play with me, and now who are starting to teach me. I know that some of the things that they do hurt, but I have also internalized the belief that this pain is for my own good, to make me stronger and to help me ascend. The regular visits from the immortals, who let me visit the celestial realms, reinforce these beliefs. I am completely unaware that the immortals are people dressed in costume, and that the celestial realms are part of a programming studio in the labs. I am still too young to learn these secrets, but one day I will, when I am so indoctrinated that learning the truth will no longer matter, other than a vague discontent inside.

I am eight years old. I have been following Mattie, Mattheo, Jerome, Carlotti and others in the labs for years. For the first year, I mainly observed, and was allowed to help change the babies and to weigh them. These are tasks I love since I love being with the babies. I enjoy smiling at them and seeing them smile back, and having them raise their little arms up to me in a gesture begging to be held. I love holding them.

As I got older, I was allowed to do more and more. After all, the expectation is that by the time I am an adult (age 12 in the Order), I will be able to fulfill the role of a trainer. While I will continue learning for the rest of my life, I will have all of the essential skills in place within a few more years.

In order to become a trainer, I have had to study physics, physiology, biochemistry, and human psychology and behavior in my classes in the school.

I go to the labs, dressed in the typical loose scrubs that everyone working in the labs wears, including the children in training. I place my hand and eyes on the biometric security scan, and give the code verbally, which is changed daily. In the morning, Mattie told me today's code, and I know that she and other fathers have told the other children who help in the labs the code as well. I pause at the small altar at the entrance to the lab where daily sacrifices are done, and prick my finger and place a small drop of blood on it. This, or some type of sacrifice, is required when entering these labs that have a figurine of the goddess Shiva to whom the labs are dedicated, over the entrance.

As I walk into the lab, I see that a 12-year-old child is going to be assessed in what we call "tune ups": instead of new programming, this child will have his programming checked for any degradation or fading. If any is detected, he will have to have those areas reprogrammed.

I am to help with the assessment today. I place the preteen in a special chair and tighten the straps on hands, feet and body. I also lower what looks like a small helmet shaped hood over his head. Mattie is there and we start.

She turns on the equipment and a readout of his brain activity shows up on a screen above him. This readout shows how much activity is occurring in various brain areas and is much more complex and thorough than an EEG; it is more like an extremely sophisticated functional MRI, with 3D readouts in various colors of various parameters of brain activity.

As Mattie watches, I ask the child simple assessment questions to start with, such as "Are you having any nightmares?" "Are you eating well?" As questions start to go a bit deeper, she takes over. "Are you happy with your schedule right now?" she asks in a gentle voice. He responds "Yes".

She then turns to me, and says, "What do you see on the brain scans?" I have been taught to read them, and I see that there is no activity that would show unhappiness and tell her this.

She then asks the child, "Is there a father you are unhappy with?"

Suddenly, on the scan, a red area lights up in the limbic area and other brain areas associated with anger and other intense emotions. I read the scans for a while, and Mattie asks, "What do you see on the scans?"

"This question elicited increased brain activity in the emotional centers, indicating that he is probably angry with someone," I say.

Mattie calls out a part named "Mind" who is able to communicate for many parts inside and asks, "Mind, who is Daniel angry with? Can you let us know what happened?"

Mind then factually narrates the events that occurred a few days ago that had caused Daniel to become angry with one of the fathers. He felt that the father was unfair in his discipline for a small prank that Daniel had done. Mind talks about Daniel in the third person, saying "He" when referring to Daniel who is the cult host; Mind sees himself as separate from the other parts that make up Daniel.

"Thank you, Mind, for sharing this information. I will try to help Daniel, and so will Lucia," Mattie says. "You are helping us to help him, and I appreciate it." Mind is then asked to go back inside, and Mattie talks to the cult host.

"I know that you feel that Father Peter is unfair at times," she says. Daniel flushes a bit but does not disagree. She continues, "I want to help you address this by learning to communicate better with him. I think we should go together to see him and find out why he was so strict with you. If he was being unfair, I will stand up for you."

Daniel looks relieved. He knows that Mattie, and in fact, all of the trainers, never make empty promises. One of the rules of the lab is that we must try to always be honest with the people we work with. Otherwise, we cannot ask them to trust us, and an individual that does not trust will be less programmable.

Mattie then turns to me and asks another question, treating me like an adult. This is part of my learning. "How do you think we should approach Father Peter?"

"I think we should first see if there are any videos of the event, including the prank and the discipline, and review them first, to see what happened, before meeting with him," I say. "He will have his opinion of the event; Daniel has his, but the videos can provide important information."

"Good," Mattie says. "Always have as much information at hand as possible. Then what?"

"Then, I would try to find a time when Father Peter is free, and schedule time to meet with him first to discuss the incident. Then, possibly the next day, bring Daniel in, letting him know that if he feels a father is unfair, it is okay to discuss this and to try to resolve the issue."

"Good," Mattie says. "Let's go look at the videos."

We unstrap Daniel, and let him go to lunch, realizing that until we have dealt with his anger and sense of having been unfairly treated, it will be difficult to do further work with him. Part of our assessment has been of his communication skills, and ability to deal with conflict. At the age of 12, while Daniel has adult responsibilities, he may still hesitate to discuss his conflicts with an adult. Our goal is to help him navigate this and learn to do so well.

After reviewing the videos, Mattie and I both agree that Father Peter was a bit harsh the other day; perhaps he was tired, or having a bad day, but we will meet with him later in the day and discuss the incident. Fathers cannot be unfair, even when they are having bad days, or they will not gain the trust and respect of those they mentor and work with. His treatment of Daniel must be addressed and Daniel must have the support needed to share how he feels, and to resolve his feelings of anger. While the technical aspects of the equipment used in the labs are interesting, I am most interested in trying to strategize and solve the complex problems that can arise when human beings interact with each other.

I am ten years old, and Mattie comes over to me at the lab. She and I look at the computerized, real-time graphs on a monitor of one of the six-month old infants, baby Maria.

"She seems to be failing," I say with some dismay. I hate it when an infant fails to thrive which is often due to the extreme stress they are placed under with the intense programming they undergo during their first year of life. It is obvious that Maria is starting to fail. She has lost weight the past few days, is not eating normally, and in the video display I pull up, she has a sad, listless look in her eyes. She is not interacting or playing with the other babies and is slow to respond even to her trainers.

"What should we do?" Mattie asks. She wants me to share what I have learned, and to implement the plan of care that I will outline if it is correct; she will correct me if I am wrong, but this is rare by now. We almost always agree in our assessments and strategies at this point, and she is giving me more and more responsibility.

"She needs time off to rest and interaction with those she is most closely bonded to; she needs to interact with her twins, and have special nurturing by the fathers she loves most."

Mattie nods. "I agree. What else?" "We need to monitor her very carefully these next few days. She is in a dangerous time, and we can't assume that the interventions will cause her to thrive. But our assessments need to be done carefully and surreptitiously; we can weigh her in her bed and do remote brain scans to see how she is responding. I would also give her extra time in the chairs, being held and rocked, and nursed, by her birth mother (the woman who has the role of being Maria's birthmother, since the original one died at her birth)," I say.

"I agree," Mattie says. "Note the interventions in her schedule and let's start."

I call up by voice the chart and schedule for Maria and tell the computer to cancel all training and to put in the bonding and nurturing interventions, as well as extra weighing and brain scanning for the next two days. Everything in the labs is computerized, and as I watch, Maria's schedule changes, including swapping the trainers who were working with her this week with the two fathers she is most bonded to, as well as special sessions with her birth mother. The fathers and birth mother will have their own schedules updated as well to reflect the changes and will not need to be told why. They can review Maria's chart on their mini tablets and will see that she is starting to fail, and will understand. This is considered a priority because we do not want to lose any babies, so the changes are started immediately.

I go and get Maria's twin sister and twin brother and place them in the crib with Maria. The two of them are overjoyed to be together with her, and they sit and smile at her. Maria looks at them, and her expression is a little less listless. I hope that they and the others who nurture her will bring her back to feeling better.

Later that day, Mattie sees me checking Maria's video display for the umpteenth time.

"Don't worry, she will probably be fine," she says. She sits down next to me, looks me in the eyes, and says, "I know how hard this is. I care, too. I love Maria. But we can only do our best and hope she responds. You can't will her to be better; she has to want to live."

I wonder how Mattie knows that I have been trying to theta Maria with "live!" entreaties. But this is Mattie, one of the people I am closest to on earth, i.e., one of my primary trainers. Of course, she knows what I am doing.

"You are forbidden to look at her videos or charts for the next ten hours," Mattie tells me. "Go and do something else for a while." Easier said than done, but she is trying to teach me to distance myself a bit and to not get overinvolved which is difficult.

The next morning, I see that the birthmother has put Maria in a baby sling, much as she did when Maria was younger. Maria looks happier and is even nursing a bit. I think she will get over her failure to thrive and I am glad. I know I am a bit too attached, I care too much, but I love each of the babies, and want them to do well, and to live.

It never occurs to me that years ago, a team of trainers looked at my own failure to thrive and treated me the same way. That is a distant memory buried in a tunnel deep in my own system.

These memories describe the multifaceted process of a young child being trained to be a programmer while growing up in a training facility. First, the adults model the behaviors, allowing even tiny children to watch, then do assessments and simple infant programming. As the child becomes older, they are allowed to ask questions, and then when they are yet older, they are asked questions designed to stimulate strategic thinking and planning.

By the age of eight, most children in the training facility in Rome have basic programming skills. By this age, children are allowed to begin helping to train and plan the training for an infant, carefully supervised by an adult trainer. They have already had several years of being allowed to observe, and then practice the skills and thought processes needed. Not all children will show great aptitude, though. Those who do are marked as having the potential to be head trainers one day.

These children are given special intense mentoring by the facility top trainers.

By the time they are age twelve, the children with the most aptitude are highly skilled trainers. Considered an adult in the Order, they are allowed to develop training plans for the infants. When they become a father in a year and a half after coming of age, they will be assigned an infant to be bonded to them, and then each year will begin training other infants. Thus, the cycle of abuse continues with each generation, in a world where this is the "norm" for the children born and raised in the facility.

In the Order, no one has a concept of a life in which abuse and programming are not "normal". It took me many years after leaving the cult (trying several times until finally leaving permanently) to adjust to the "outside" world. I had to learn a whole new worldview, one that many parts distrusted and disbelieved deeply in at first: the possibility that life could be lived without the constant expectation of high performance, or without the shadow of constant, terrible abuse.

This adjustment was made more difficult by a world outside the facility where the majority of people I encountered did not understand – or seem to even want to understand - what I had been through. I shared just small parts of my story at churches I attended, and people acted frightened of me and avoided me. I shared small parts of my story with counselors, and they stopped answering calls to schedule an appointment; another told me that abuse like this is normal, and that it was normal to lose time (have memory gaps). I had to look for another counselor who would not try to normalize torture and amnesia, who I assumed was probably part of a cult herself.

The individuals who could listen to my story and not run were very few and far between, and often charged high fees for this listening. These were fees that were difficult to afford.

I learned to stop sharing my story at the new church I started attending, and people were not afraid of me. I learned to stop telling friends about my past, and the new friends I made did not avoid me. The outside world, the world outside the facility, by its own modeling and behavior, taught me to be silent if I wanted acceptance and to not be feared.

This rejection by those without a cult background is the reality that many survivors face. I did not have survivor friends by choice – all of the survivor friends that I made early in my healing had a mission of drawing me back to my handlers, just as I (unknowingly, but destructively all the same) had the same mission towards them. We understood and did not fear, and accepted each other, all too well, because the kind presenters in the front did not realize that we were all still cult active.

So as healing and awareness increased over time, without survivor friends, I had extremely few options for friendships outside of the facility, a facility filled with the people I loved dearly, people I had grown up with and bonded to for years. People that the cult was *threatening to torture to death if I did not return to Rome.*

I am grateful for the three friends that I was able to make over a period of thirty years, who were not cult members, who were not dissociative, and who helped me immensely during my own healing journey. They learned my story gradually, and I was friends with two for years before they heard my story. Each offered me accountability and safety for a time, a gift without measure in a world that all too often seems to treat the survivor trying to break free as an adult as if their pain, grief and trauma are their fault, unbelievable, or something to be avoided knowing about. I am also grateful for the counselors (whose high fees were more than worth it), and prayer ministers who have also helped me during my healing journey. I will always be grateful for the gift that each has given me, simply by not abandoning me when I shared my pain with them.

But even then, I had to deal with the expectations of the kind helpers from a world that cannot understand what it is like to grow up in a facility. The expectation was that I would feel, "Oh, my gosh, thank you for helping me to be free," (I am grateful, but that took time) and that I would hate the evil cult. This "evil" was my brother who saved my life when we were hanging from a rope off of a mountainside when I was twelve years old, because of an equipment failure, and later shared a hot meal and conversation filled with laughter. This "evil" was my twin sister, the one I had sat with and whispered secrets to late at night, the sister who attended my wedding in France, the sister who played with me, wept with me, and comforted me growing up. This "evil" I was expected to reject so utterly was the fathers who held me, gave me a bottle as a baby, who comforted me when I cried, and who desperately tried to keep me alive in an extremely dangerous environment. This "evil" was my children, who I had nursed and loved for years. The face of this "evil" was the people I loved most on earth, and I could not agree that leaving the cult meant that I had to hate them.

They did not understand. And this made the healing journey so much, much harder. This is one reason I am sharing my story. For those that can hear it, perhaps it will help them understand better, even if a little, a world that seems to defy comprehension for those not born into it.

Chapter 11: Christmas in the Vatican

I am ten years old, and like all of the children, I have been looking forward to Christmas for weeks. Although we are undergoing occultic training and mind control, the Order still celebrates Christmas with extra time off, special treats (is there anything so wonderful as the flavor of marzipan, or of a rich fruitcake?), and best of all, we are allowed to make special presents and give them to those we love.

Of course, Christmas does not have the Christian trappings or connotations seen in most places that celebrate it. No crèches or nativity scenes here, and the carols and songs this time of year have instead have been adapted to carry occult meanings. "O come, O come, Emmanuel" our choirs sing poignantly, all the while being taught that we are waiting for our own messiah, "He Who Is To Come" who will bring peace and joy to the world. We are waiting for our world leader, and this song expresses our longing for his advent. "Joy to the World" is sung joyfully in anticipation of his birth.

I recall the first time I saw the painting, "The Light of the World", that hangs in the Black Pope's secret office. Painted in the mid-1800s, this enormous painting (it covers half of a wall that is fifteen feet long) shows people representing the various nations of the world, dressed surprisingly in modern dress, with hands upraised towards a blond, blue-eyed man with a charismatic gaze. This man stands at the top of the painting and receives their adoration. I have been told that this man will be born in my lifetime, and that even I could be part of bringing him into the world. All that I know is that like the other members of the Order, I look forward to his coming. When he comes, we will no longer have to be hidden behind closed doors; we and the other 12 great societies (the international occultic groups) and the Asian occultic societies, will be able to come out openly, and will be favored by him.

But that is the future, and Christmas is almost here. For months, I have been making presents for my classmates and the three fathers I love most. I have painted a picture for Danny, my brother, who loves art. I have made Lizzie a small sculpture of a house in the hills of Tuscany that she especially admired when we visited there after a training exercise. All of us children have been taught various arts and crafts as part of our development and to encourage creativity, and these gifts represent giving up precious free time to create them.

I have knit scarves for many of my classmates in their favorite colors to wear when we next have a cold weather training exercise. I have sculpted a beautiful rose for Father Jerome and tinted it with soft creams that are the colors of his rose. I have created a belt that has been tooled with engravings for Father Carlotti who I know especially likes leather. I want what I create for Mattheo to be held next to his body, so I sew a special vest in soft linen and embroider it to wear under his robe on cooler days. The embroidery is of his favorite flowers, including roses and lilies. It is so much fun to create these presents, wrap them, and then wait until Christmas day when we can give them to one another.

On Christmas day, we are all up bright and early. All the children have small boxes at the ends of their beds, and we all give cries of delight as we look in them, and take out oranges, pomegranates, dried fruit as well as nuts. We will share them with each other, because in the Order, we are taught to share with each other very young, and enjoy doing so. This is half the fun, the sharing.

I take my presents to Lizzie and Danny in their rooms. They are in a different class than mine so they sleep in their own class' dormitory. They love their presents, and then they give me mine. Danny has sculpted a small bird out of clay that he fired, and I love it. Danny especially loves birds and spends part of his free time watching them flying. Sometimes I wonder if they represent a deep, inner desire to be free from the demands and rules of the Order, but I never ask him. Some things are better left unasked. I love the bird and give him a big hug, saying "Thank you!"

Lizzie gives me her gift. She is very good at crocheting, and has crocheted me a beautiful, jaunty little cap in my favorite colors. I give her a big hug, and then I go and get my class, and we go for a special treat in the communal dining room of hot cocoa with whipped cream and waffles with berries. I have my other presents to give the fathers in a small bag with me, but I want to give them to each when we can be alone. I want this gift-giving to be a private event, even though I share most other things with others.

Later in the afternoon, I see Mattheo and run to him. "I have something for you," I tell this father I love so much.

"Let's go to my office," he says, understanding that I want to give my gift privately. We go in, and he closes the doors so that visitors will knock before entering.

I hand him my present, and his eyes tear up. He knows the time and effort it took to design this vest, and then to embroider it. I have been working on it during part of my free time, and before falling asleep at night, for the past seven months.

"I will cherish this always," he says, and puts it on and buttons the silk buttons. I am pleased, more than I can express, as I see his pleasure in this gift.

"I have something for you," he says.

I am surprised and pleased because the fathers usually never give gifts to the children. While I am his top pupil, and he has been mentoring me for years, I am still touched that he took time from his busy schedule to find me a Christmas present. I open it: it is a beautiful painting of a spot near the mountains in northern Italy that I especially love. We conducted some of our military training there this past year, and afterwards, I spent my R&R hiking the mountains and sailing the lakes surrounded by tree-covered mountains. This painting shows Danny, Lizzie and me sailing on the lake, laughing together. I realize that he has painted this for me to remind me of this happy time.

"Thank you," I say, with tears in my eyes. "I will treasure this, too."

While I am not allowed to keep personal items in my dormitory room, other than a candle and medals won for high achievement, I will store this gift from the father I love in a special storage locker I have, with items that I will one day decorate my room with when I am a father. For once I become a father myself, I will move out of the dormitory and have a room of my own, which I can decorate with personal items. This will occur in two years, and already Mattheo is trying to provide things that will help me with the transition from communal living to privacy.

I go back to the communal dining room, where at one end stands a huge Christmas tree, decorated with garlands of popcorn, fruit, candies and candles. During the day, all of us children are allowed to pick treats off of this tree, and within 24 hours it is picked nearly clean of everything except its candles. At night, we enter in and sing together, as the lit tree glows in the darkened room. It all feels holy and reverent, and I love the smell of the pine tree which has been brought in from the mountains to the north the previous day. It reminds me of hiking in the mountains that I love so much.

After singing, we have a small service. Of course, there is the evening sacrifice, and then we return to bed, to laugh and chat and remember the fun of this day.

Over the next few days, we all have a lighter-than-normal schedule, since it is the end of the year and we are preparing for a great event that will happen soon: Epiphany.

Chapter 12: The Gift of the Magi

Epiphany, or the twelfth day of Christmas, is the day that tradition says the magi brought their gifts to the Christ child. But at the Vatican training facility, the gift that is coming has nothing to do with Christianity, and everything to do with something the fathers love most: our new batch of babies.

Over the week of January 6th, the new batch of babies is born. The fertilization and implantation of the eggs are carefully timed so that the births occur during this week. While the babies are born over the week, the evening before Epiphany, the gift of the magi, is counted as the birthday of the babies born into the group. All the fathers are involved in the births and rituals following birth. The logistics and manpower required for the births and rituals is why the births are spread out over the week, rather than all occurring on January 5th.

The fathers believe that each generation of babies are the hope of the Order, and they look forward expectantly to meeting them. For months, they have been talking to the fetuses in the womb, since the birth mothers have been brought to our facility for this purpose. The fetuses have already bonded to the fathers' voices, and they are looking forward to meeting them in person.

There is an air of rushed, yet professional, expectancy as the birth mothers are prepped for the birth, and labor is started. One by one, the babies are born in careful timing, and the three fathers that the newborn will bond to first, the fathers they will love most, are present at each infant's birth. As soon as the infant is born, the birth mother is torn in two and killed, and the terrible words "You are so evil, you killed her," are spoken to the newborn. I am allowed to watch two births, and I feel funny in my stomach when I watch the birth mothers pulled apart with a special tool. The crying, wailing infant is picked up, and the father starts to suffocate it. "Only Satan can give you life. Do you wish to live?" the father says, asking the infant psychically to give permission for a demon to enter it. Most babies fight against demons entering them, but they also want to live. Most give permission, and then the father breathes into their mouth and nostrils, and the baby continues crying. I have heard (but not personally seen yet) that occasionally an infant refuses, and it ends up dying before it has taken its first breath, suffocated because of its refusal to agree to what the father asks.

I wonder why some babies agree, and some refuse, and later, I ask this question to Mattheo. "Why do some babies refuse to take the life that Satan offers them?" I ask. "Why are they so different?"

"Because some are still clinging too much to their mortality, and would rather die than become immortal," he says. "Becoming an immortal is a gift, but not all want to receive it."

"But couldn't the baby be allowed to live, anyway?" I ask. Something about this process bothers me, and my ten-year old mind is trying to understand our ways.

"No, Luce, a baby that refuses the life that Satan offers would refuse everything it was offered later on. It would be in constant pain, and would end up dying soon anyway," Mattheo says. I wonder how he knows, and wonder if in the past, they let some of the refusing babies live.

I am bothered by the birthing ceremonies, and the terrible death of the birthmothers. It stirs up something vague and uneasy deep inside, but I have already forgotten my own similar birth. I have also had years of the fathers explaining to me why it is necessary that the birthmother dies. In spite of their explanations couched in occultic theology, it still feels wrong, deep inside.

But the next morning, the fun begins. Mattheo has assigned me to be a helper with two of the babies that he will be a primary trainer to. While I cannot be a primary trainer until I am a full father, right now I can be a helper, and I love attending these helpless, soft, red and wrinkled little babies. They spend a lot of time sleeping, but I help change them, take them to the female fathers who nurse them, and help make baby slings so that the fathers can carry the babies around as they work. These babies have had a traumatic time in the womb, and during birth, and the fathers are careful to nurture these babies and provide lots of love during the first few weeks of life. There will be training sessions started, of course; but I love simply gazing at the babies, watching them blink, squint and yawn, and place a finger inside their tiny hands. I am always surprised at how strong their grasp is, for such a tiny little being.

I help to weigh the babies and assess them; I have learned these and many other skills in the past ten years of training and can do lots of tasks and help identify any problems or unusual events that occur. These babies, born on Epiphany, really do feel like a gift, even though no magi have brought them to the labs. Instead, they have been brought in on schedule within the wombs of their unfortunate birthmothers, who will never hold or be able to speak to these precious little babies.

Because the children in the order are conceived in a laboratory, the timing of birth can be timed quite precisely, especially with drugs that can induce labor. These births are anticipated with great excitement each year, and the entire schedule for that week will be designed to assign fathers and babies to one another for the process of bonding and attachment outside the womb, to augment that which was already done while the baby was inside the birthmother. The children who are 13 and have completed the coming of age ceremony (see next chapter) are especially excited, because now they will be allowed to mentor a baby of their own and train it.

Chapter 13: Coming of Age

I am twelve years old, and I have just finished my schooling at the end of my twelfth year. I am no longer in school and am spending my days working in the programming labs, helping teach some of the younger children, and doing other tasks, while also living for several weeks in each of my hosting presentations around the world. Months pass as I work in my role as a young trainer and help to teach the younger children in their classes. I also help with planning military training exercises for the younger children, along with my classmates. We are all busy, and several months pass by quickly.

Finally, early summer comes, when I am thirteen years and a half years old. Today is a day that I have looked forward to for years: the day that I become a father in the Jesuit Order. After today, I will have traded my brown acolyte robes and rope belt for the black robes of a father. Instead of being addressed as "Luce", I will be addressed as "Father Luke", for all fathers in the order have male names, even though their birth names reflect their real gender.

The rest of my class is as excited and nervous as I am. I know that the other classes feel the same way. We wander and talk aimlessly, but mostly are quiet, waiting to go to the place where our lives will change forever.

Soon, Mattheo and the other fathers come, and signal to us that it is time to go. We get into a van and drive to the shore. We then are taken by boat to an island off the coast of Italy. This island is owned by the Order and is never visited by those outside of the Order. There is excellent security by air, land and water so intruders cannot land there; they will be stopped long before they reach its shores.

The other three classes are there, along with mine. Each class will go to a different part of the island. Our class lines up in an area that is filled with golden painted poles. On each pole is tied a human being, of varying ages, between newborn and octogenarian elderly, pregnant mothers, and whole families. There are cries and moans on the wind from the individuals who are tied up, waiting, for what, they do not know.

But I know. This is a special ceremony, a very special ritual, which each father must undergo before joining the order. At the edge of the field, I am given a golden knife, and each of my classmates is also given one. There are one thousand people tied to poles, and the field looks like a harvest crop of human beings, humans whose hair blows softly in the breeze, humans whose soft cries of bewilderment and fear are carried towards me. I hear the cries of the babies and toddlers, who dislike being tied in place. They sound fretful now, but I know that their cries will change soon. I have watched this ceremony before as a spectator sitting in a curved raised area that surrounds part of this enormous field.

There are tables with golden chalices, and as instructed, my classmates and I each pick one up. We wait. An opening chant of praise to Satan and other deities is done. This day and each of us are dedicated to them; the chant asks these beings to give us the strength to do what we must today.

Then, a golden tone sounds, and as instructed, we begin. I begin killing people, slashing their throats, trying to be quick so that their screams and hoarse cries are cut off quickly. One by one, I go down a row, killing, slashing, and collecting some of the blood in my chalice. When it is full, I go to a huge bronze bowl, and pour the blood in, where it mixes with an anti-clotting powder that is stirred by helpers who stand nearby.

I continue killing, because this sacrifice is the gift that I must give to the immortals to prove that I am ready to become a father. It is a warm day, and soon I am sweating, but I continue; a baby is quickly killed, the blood gathered; then a child, then an elderly lady. With each death, I am feeling more and more tired; I feel an exhaustion that cannot be explained by the physical act. I am feeling inside of me the weight of these deaths. I feel depressed and saddened, but I must continue.

I go down another line, and kill and collect blood from 1, 2, 3, 4, 5, 6, 7, 8, 9, 10 people of all ages. By now, the adults are screaming as they realize what is happening, and the infants are wailing at the top of their lungs. The toddlers are screaming as well. I am so tired. I go to a table, where I am given watered wine by one of the helpers, as I am hot, thirsty, and want my senses dulled; doing this killing is starting to feel unbearable, but I know that I must continue if I want to become a father.

Mechanically, I continue, going down another line of people: 11, 12, 13, 14, 15, 16, 17, 18, 19, 20, collecting the blood from each. I am feeling heavy and as if a great weight is pressing me down: death has a weight, and I am feeling it. I look around, and see my classmates looking tired and haggard, just as I do. I wonder if we will all make it through.

I take another drink of the watered wine. One of the helpers, an older father, whispers encouragement to me. "You are doing well, you can do this," he says.

I go back and continue killing another line of people. This time, I kill the babies first; I can't stand to hear their screaming wails. After that, I kill the toddlers, and then the adults. 21, 22, 23, 24, 25, 26, 27, 28, 29, 30, 31, 32, 33, 34, 35, collecting the blood from each and pouring it into the large basin. I am starting to feel numb; it feels as if my arms, legs and heart are turning into stone. I have killed before, but never so many at one time, and my limbs feel heavier and heavier. I go back and get more watered wine; I wipe my face, neck and hands with a watered towel, wondering if I will ever feel clean again; this goes deeper than the skin.

I continue, working my way down the lines: 36, 37, 38, 39...59, collecting and pouring blood, taking rests. I am aware that the helpers there who help me wipe my face and hands, who provide me with drinks when I am thirsty, are also helping keep careful count of how many people we have each killed. I know that I must kill 84 people today; others in my class will kill either 83 or 84, but we must together kill all of the people on this field. But I am tired, so tired. I am sad, so sad. I don't want to keep going.

"Keep going," the helper whispers to me. "You don't have that many more." I look at him and wonder how he made it through his own coming of age ceremony. But this feels less like a ceremony, and more like...a killing field...this is how I think of this, secretly, inside. I am at a killing field, and I feel like a killing machine instead of a human being.

I keep going. 60, 61, 62, 63...I am now up to 80, I have slashed, stabbed and gathered blood from so many. I am splattered with blood myself. I have trouble lifting the knife, I am so weary. All I want is to lay down, and never get up again. I wonder if anyone has died from the crushing weight of so many deaths, from this act of merciless slaying of others who cannot fight back. I hate myself, utterly, and think about turning the knife on myself. I know that the helpers are there, watching carefully, monitoring us to prevent such acts. I see my "helper" coming closer to me, as if he can discern my thoughts. Sighing, I go over and take another drink of watered wine. I am a little drunk by now, but not incapacitated. I need this numbing, and once again, I take up my knife and continue. 81, collect the blood in my chalice; 82, collect the blood; 83, collect the blood, 84, collect the blood. I am done. I have finished. I have killed 84 people today, and I take my chalice and for the final time, I pour the blood into the container.

"Good, good, congratulations, Father Luke!" the helper says. I see Mattheo, Jerome, and Carlotti coming over as well to congratulate me.

But I don't care. I am filled with an utter, utter self-hatred of myself for being capable of this act. I am filled with a deep despair, and I fall down, completely spent. I can no longer stand and give in to the deep weariness and crushing sense of weight that I feel: the blood guilt of so many people killed for no reason other than this sacrifice was "demanded" by beings that I increasingly hate for these, and other demands.

But I cannot say this out loud. It would break the hearts of the fathers I love, who come over to me. "Congratulations, Father Luke!" they each say in turn. For months, I have longed to hear myself called this name; it is the culmination of 13 years of intense training and effort. But I no longer care what I am called. I just want to lay down and die.

The fathers gather around me and help me to a bench where I lay down. They seem to understand how difficult this is for me. Through half-closed eyes, I watch as my other classmates are continuing. I am the first to finish, but Conner finishes soon after, then Mary Margaret, then Timothy, and soon the others are done. Our class has completed the killings, but like me, they are all exhausted and depleted, and are laying down as well.

I know that there will be a special banquet tonight in our honor. We will be given our black robes, and for the first time each of us will wear a rose pinned to our black robes, and will be called by our father names. But I do not really care anymore. I wonder if it is worth it and decide that it is not.

I hate the name "Father Luke" deep inside beneath conscious thought, because I realize that the cost has been too high. Today, I lost an important part of myself, and the senseless killing has made me realize that I have done what I hate and abhor, but I was too frightened to say "no". I was too conditioned from a lifetime of training in obedience to say, "This is insane!", too loyal to those I love to break their hearts. But today, at the killing field, my heart has been broken, and something very important — the humanity inside — has been irrevocably broken as well. I will never forgive the people I have loved for bringing me to this point, and placing me in this unbearable situation to carry out this intolerable act.

I am thirteen years old — still a child — but I feel very old, very weary, as if the weight of the world and my own sin, is on my shoulders. Oh, I will pretend tonight that I am happy - I will smile and act accordingly. I will continue to show how proud I am of my black robes and of being a father in the Order.

But I also realize that I deeply, deeply want to become free of this. I have just become a father, and I realize that I want to leave.

I understand that a coming of age ritual described as above may seem unbelievable to some. When this memory returned, I reeled for weeks from it. The sheer amount of death, the lack of value for human life, staggered me as the feelings, the taste of watered wine in my mouth, the heat and exhaustion of that day, feeling the stickiness of blood and its itch, returned. How I wish that this was fiction, and not a memory!

However, this is indeed how the Jesuits turn a young teen into a full father: by destroying part of the child's humanity. By having them participate in something so grievous, so terrible, that creates such guilt, that the mind cannot endure it, which ensures ongoing secrecy and that the vows of silence and loyalty will never be broken.

"We know what you are, and only we can love you," as the fathers tell the child frequently when growing up, and during reprogramming as they become adults, seems all too believable after going through this terrible ceremony. It feels very, very true that no one who has not been part of this evil could ever truly accept the child who has participated in this. It took me a very long time to realize that the God of the Bible could forgive this — even this. That I was not destined for hell because I had done this when I was still a child. But He does forgive even this, and more, because of the gift of His Son, Jesus, who bore all of this guilt on Himself when He died on the cross.

That is great love. That is great mercy, mercy beyond understanding. But it is real.

Chapter 14: Wedded to Satan

I am thirteen years old, just three months after becoming a full father. I am now called "Father Luke" by others (although in private, those closest to me still call me Luce). In public, I call Danny, Lizzie, Conner, Mary Margaret, Timothy, Andrew and others by their father names. There is another ceremony to go through today, a ceremony that I have been carefully prepared for years, by the fathers. A ceremony that I have carefully fasted and purified myself for. Today is my wedding day.

It is evening on a day when the air is warm but a soft breeze carries the smell of flowers on it. I am standing at one end of a wooded grove that has a long pathway down the middle, a pathway that is covered by a red silken carpet. On each side of the path stand men and women in their best dress. The women are dressed in top designer gowns with full skirts. Each person is carrying a lit candle in their hands. The multitude of jewels covering the women's dresses twinkle in the candlelight.

The men are in full evening dress, including vests, top hats, bow ties and long tailed jackets. Their lit candles are reflected in the shine of their suits. These men and women are leaders of the twelve occultic societies, as well as carefully selected world leaders who have been initiated generationally into the secrets of the occult world, and they are here as honored guests at my wedding.

Today, I will marry Satan.

I am dressed in a beautiful wedding dress of purest white, and a golden circlet that rests on my head. I am wearing diamonds everywhere. They are scattered in my hair, and I wear diamond bracelets on my wrists, diamond anklets, and diamond necklaces that sparkles in the candlelight. My curly hair is gathered up, with loose tendrils falling along the sides of my face.

I am excited and nervous. I am holding a beautiful bouquet of white roses in my hands, which are tightly clenched. Up on a raised dais, I see Theo, the beautiful form of Satan, who is awaiting me. His black hair and eyes shine in the candlelight, and he is dressed in a formal black tuxedo. He glances at me, and I tremble with adoration. Maria, the part who is in love with Theo, is out. She has been prepared since earliest childhood for this ceremony and anticipates becoming his bride.

Her name, Maria, signifies her role as a spiritual being in my system. This part is a celestial mother figure whom the Order hopes will be able to achieve the highest honor a female mortal can: bearing Satan's child. In the Order's theology, this child will be the much longed for and hoped for "light of the world", a world leader over the coming New World Order. Christians have dubbed him "antichrist" but this is not what the Order calls him. They call him "anointed one".

An organ sitting on a stone platform behind me begins softly playing the strains of "Ave Maria". This is my wedding song, and for the rest of my life, will be one of my system's biggest triggers, a reminder of the day I became Satan's wife.

Of course, I understand that Satan has several wives; he is a polygamist. Mary Margaret will also be wed to him, and Lizzie, and other female fathers, fathers deemed worthy of this high honor because of their participation in the coming of age ceremony, which is in essence a huge sacrifice to Satan. I also know that he weds women from various occultic groups around the world. But today, it is my day.

There have been sacrifices all day long, starting at dawn. And now I, a mere mortal, will be in a sense another sacrifice. I will join my mortal body with this being. For the oracles have foretold that the light of the world's entrance to the mortal realms would be linked to me. How, we are not sure, but this wedding is part of the hope.

The soft strains of the organ swell, and at a measured pace, Mattheo, the father I love most, holds my arm gently and walks me down the aisle. As we pass by, the guests lining the sides of the pathway bow in honor to me. Then, we approach the dais, and Mattheo turns and stands close to it below the steps, while I slowly walk up the steps to the platform above to meet Theo.

His smile is beautiful and charming, and his eyes look like two polished onyx stones, deep and black.

He takes my hand, and I say my wedding vows to him, promising to love and serve him forever, to never forsake my love for him. I bow before him, kiss his feet, and then I turn and do a sacrifice on an altar that is near us both.

Then, Theo takes me in his arms and carries me to a large white bed that is located on the dais. It is in full view of all of the guests, and in this public place, under the watchful eyes of all, Theo rapes me, slowly and painfully, over and over again.

After a while, I pass out from the emotional, physical and spiritual pain. I go unconscious, but this is not uncommon. Human beings do not like being physically and spiritually assaulted by the demonic, and this is an extreme assault.

It is the next morning, and Mattheo gently wakes me. I have been unconscious all night. Jerome, Carlotti, Lizzie and Dannie are there with me.

"You did well," Mattheo says. I realize that this means he is glad that I survived a ceremony that has killed others.

"I love you," Lizzie says. I embrace her. I feel exhausted and can barely raise my head off of the bed.

"You were beautiful last night," says Jerome.

Today, I am dressed in a silk nightgown, so someone undressed me and washed the blood off. I lost a lot of blood the night before; I can feel the special weakness that means that I am drained and anemic.

Dannie, ever thoughtful Dannie, hands me a cup of broth filled with nutrients. He smiles quietly at me, but I see the sadness that flashes for just a moment in my brother's eyes. He knows, and I know, that I will never be quite the same again. I love him for understanding how sad this makes me, too. I smile quietly back and sip the broth. But inside, I am planning my escape, an escape that I now realize that I must make. Because last night made me realize that if I do not, the sheer evil that I have encountered could kill me – even me – strong as I am.

Ten months later, I try to escape the Order for the first time.

Afterword

This book has been about my memories from the first 13 ½ years of growing up in the Jesuit Order. It is not all my memories, but only the ones that I felt would best illustrate what it was like. The most important thing that my memories illustrate is the intentional use of attachment and bonding by the Jesuit fathers who raised me, and its impact on me over a lifetime. It is terrible, indeed, when a young child who has no other alternative for escape is forced to bond to abusers who themselves were raised in an evil environment. For the child will bond in order to survive. My hope is that this book will show the necessity for those who support survivors to provide safe, healthy relationships, and to help the survivor to grow in the skills needed to develop such relationships with many others. By relationships, I do not mean "re-parenting", because that is not possible; I only mean 'relationships' – friendships with healthy, non-dissociative people who accept the survivor regardless of their past.

I believe that the lifetime of bonding and attachment between cult members from the earliest childhood, as I describe in my book, is one of the main issues that makes it very difficult for people to leave highly organized cults. If an individual attempts to leave the cult, which means in groups such as the Order, leaving father, mother, sister, brother, children and closest friends, the question is then legitimately raised: *Leave for what? Who will love the survivor who is getting free, a freedom that involves breaking off with those the survivor has loved for a lifetime?* Understanding and answering these questions in a safe, healthy way is one thing that I believe could promote more individuals leaving the many organized cult groups that manipulate attachment needs.

About the Author

Since 1999, svali has written articles and led online groups to help educate survivors and the public regarding dissociation, ritual abuse, mind control and the work of organized occult groups internationally. Her articles and free book (*Breaking the Chain*) have been translated into five languages and read by both survivors and therapists around the world. Her book about how programming is done and suggestions on how to heal, *It's Not Impossible*, has been used by survivors, therapists, prayer ministers and those who support survivors from around the world to gain a greater understanding of these topics.

A former trainer for an international occultic group, she left the group sixteen years ago, and currently helps to educates others about topics related to ritual abuse and mind control through articles and podcast interviews.

You can learn more about svali and read other articles she has written on her blog:

svalispeaks again.wordpress.com.

Made in United States
Troutdale, OR
04/25/2025

30901337R00176